CALCULUS

GRAPHICAL, NUMERICAL, ALGEBRAIC

ADVANCED PLACEMENT CORRELATIONS AND PREPARATION

PEARSON

Prentice Hall

Needham, Massachusetts
Upper Saddle River, New Jersey

This publication provides correlations, AB and BC assignment guides, worksheets, and sample tests that will help you prepare a course that is equivalent to a college calculus course. Also included are **Pacing Guides** for the AB and BC courses. Lesson plans and correlations are available on the World Wide Web at www.phschool.com.

Concepts Worksheets provide additional work on important calculus ideas that often give students trouble.

Group Activity Explorations provide opportunities for more Cooperative Learning.

The **Assignment Guides** in this publication differ from those in the Teacher's Guide in that they are more focused on the AB and BC courses. Problems that are listed under Preparation for Advanced Placement exam can be used for review for the exam.

ISBN 0-13-067821-X

6 7 8 9 10   07 06 05 04

CONTENTS

A Functions, Graphs, and Limits

	Pages
1. Analysis of graphs	throughout
2. Limits of functions (including one-sided limits)	
a. Calculating limits using algebra	57–59, 61
b. Estimating limits from graphs or tables of data	56–57, 59–61, 65–66, 71, 74–78, 135, 419–422
3. Asymptotic and unbounded behavior	
a. Understanding asymptotes in terms of graphical behavior	65–66, 69–71
b. Describing asymptotic behavior in terms of limits involving infinity	65–71
c. Comparing relative magnitudes of functions and their rates of change	69–71, 425–430
4. Continuity as a property of functions	
a. Understanding continuity in terms of limits	74–78
b. Geometric understanding of graphs of continuous functions (Intermediate Value Theorem and Extreme Value Theorem)	73–79, 177–179

B Derivatives

	Pages
1. Concept of the derivative	
a. Derivative defined as the limit of the difference quotient	95–97, 100, 105–106, 113–116, 135, 164, 277–278
b. Relationship between differentiability and continuity	106, 109–110
2. Derivative at a point	
a. Slope of a curve at a point	83–86, 95, 97–98, 114–115, 118, 124, 138–139, 144–145, 150–151, 157–158, 162, 165–167, 187, 398
b. Tangent line to a curve at a point and local linear approximation	83–86, 106–107, 114–115, 118, 124, 138–139, 144–145, 150–152, 157–158, 162, 165–167, 186–187, 220–222, 225–226, 398
c. Instantaneous rate of change as the limit of average rate of change	55–56, 82–83, 86–87, 122, 124, 128
d. Approximate rate of change from graphs and tables of values	82–83, 98–100
3. Derivative as a function	
a. Corresponding characteristics of graphs of f and f'	97–98, 188–189, 194–197, 199, 201–203
b. Relationship between the increasing and decreasing behavior of f and the sign of f'	187–189, 194–197, 199, 201–203
c. The Mean Value Theorem and its geometric consequences	186–190
d. Equations involving derivatives	122–123, 126, 190–191, 233–236, 304–305, 309–312, 330–331, 333, 335, 342–346
4. Second derivatives	
a. Corresponding characteristics of the graphs of f, f', and f''	197–203
b. Relationship between the concavity of f and the sign of f''	197–199, 201–202
c. Points of inflection as places where concavity changes	198–203

	Pages
5. Applications of derivatives	
a. Analysis of curves, including the notions of monotonicity and concavity	179–183, 187–189, 194–203
b. Optimization, both absolute (global) and relative (local) extrema	177, 179–183, 194–197, 200–203, 206–213
c. Modeling rates of change, including related rates problems	232–236
d. Use of implicit differentiation to find the derivative of an inverse function	158–160, 166, 169
e. Interpretation of derivative as a rate of change in varied applied contexts, including velocity, speed, and acceleration	122–129, 136–137, 143, 160, 164–166, 187, 190–191, 198–200, 232–236, 304, 309–312, 330–337, 342–346
6. Computation of derivatives	
a. Knowledge of derivatives of basic functions, including x^r, exponential, trigonometric, and inverse trigonometric functions	112–113, 117–118, 134–136, 138, 153–154, 157–161, 163–169
b. Basic rules for the derivative of sums, products, and quotients of functions	113–118, 136
c. Chain rule and implicit differentiation	141–146, 149–154, 168

C Integrals

	Pages
1. Riemann sums	
a. Concept of a Riemann sum over equal subdivisions	247–253, 260–262, 264–265, 271, 364–370, 374–375, 383, 387, 395–397, 402–404
b. Computation of Riemann sums using left, right, and midpoint evaluation points	248–253

	Pages
2. Interpretations and properties of definite integrals	
a. Definite integral as a limit of Riemann sums	258–265, 271, 364–370, 374–375, 383, 387, 395–397, 402–404
b. Definite integral of the rate of change of a quantity over an interval interpreted as the change of the quantity over the interval: $$\int_a^b f'(x)\,dx = f(b) - f(a)$$	363–370
c. Basic properties of definite integrals	268–270
3. Applications of integrals	262–263, 265, 270–272, 283–285, 309–312, 325, 363–370, 374–379, 383–389, 395–398, 401–407, 440–441
4. Fundamental Theorem of Calculus	
a. Use of the Fundamental Theorem to evaluate definite integrals	282–285 (and throughout from here on)
b. Use of the Fundamental Theorem to represent a particular antiderivative, and the analytical and graphical analysis of functions so defined	272–274 (exploratory), 277–282, 308, 316
5. Techniques of antidifferentiation	
a. Antiderivatives following directly from derivatives of basic functions	190–191, 283–285, 307–309
b. Antiderivatives by substitution of variables (including change of limits for definite integrals)	315–320
6. Applications of antidifferentiation	
a. Finding specific antiderivatives using initial conditions, including applications to motion along a line	190–191, 280, 303, 309–312, 363–365, 367
b. Solving separable differential equations and using them in modeling	304–305, 320–321, 330–337, 342–346 (exponential growth in precalculus framework 20–23)
7. Numerical approximations to definite integrals	247–253, 265–266 (numerical integration using calculator occurs throughout from here on), 289–294

A Functions, Graphs, and Limits

	Pages
1. Analysis of graphs	throughout
2. Limits of functions (including one-sided limits)	
a. Calculating limits using algebra	57–59, 61
b. Estimating limits from graphs or tables of data	56–57, 59–61, 65–66, 71, 74–78, 135, 419–422
3. Asymptotic and unbounded behavior	
a. Understanding asymptotes in terms of graphical behavior	65–66, 69–71
b. Describing asymptotic behavior in terms of limits involving infinity	65–71
c. Comparing relative magnitudes of functions and their rates of change	69–71, 425–430
4. Continuity as a property of functions	
a. Understanding continuity in terms of limits	74–78
b. Geometric understanding of graphs of continuous functions (Intermediate Value Theorem and Extreme Value Theorem)	73–79, 177–179
5. Parametric, polar, and vector functions	127, 144–145, 513–517, 529–534, 536, 539–548, 552–557 (precalculus), 559–561, 564 (parametric functions in precalculus framework 26–29, 35)

B Derivatives

	Pages
1. Concept of the derivative	
a. Derivative defined as the limit of the difference quotient	95–97, 100, 105–106, 113–116, 135, 164, 277–278
b. Relationship between differentiability and continuity	106, 109–110
2. Derivative at a point	
a. Slope of a curve at a point	83–86, 95, 97–98, 114–115, 118, 124, 138–139, 144–145, 150–151, 157–158, 162, 165–167, 187, 398, 559–561
b. Tangent line to a curve at a point and local linear approximation	83–86, 106–107, 114–115, 118, 124, 138–139, 144–145, 150–152, 157–158, 162, 165–167, 186–187, 220–222, 225–226, 398, 532–534, 560–561
c. Instantaneous rate of change as the limit of average rate of change	55–56, 82–83, 86–87, 122, 124, 128
d. Approximate rate of change from graphs and tables of values	82–83, 98–100
3. Derivative as a function	
a. Corresponding characteristics of graphs of f and f'	97–98, 188–189, 194–197, 199, 201–203
b. Relationship between the increasing and decreasing behavior of f and the sign of f	187–189, 194–197, 199, 201–203
c. The Mean Value Theorem and its geometric consequences	186–190
d. Equations involving derivatives	122–123, 126, 190–191, 233–236, 304–305, 309–312, 330–331, 333, 335, 342–346
4. Second derivatives	
a. Corresponding characteristics of the graphs of f, f', and f''	197–203
b. Relationship between the concavity of f and the sign of f''	197–199, 201–202
c. Points of inflection as places where concavity changes	198–203

	Pages
5. Applications of derivatives	
a. Analysis of curves, including the notions of monotonicity and concavity	179–183, 187–189, 194–203
b. Analysis of planar curves given in parametric form, polar form, and vector form, including velocity and acceleration vectors	127, 144–145, 513–517, 529–534, 536, 539–548, 552–557 (precalculus), 559–561, 564 (parametric functions in precalculus framework 26–29, 35)
c. Optimization, both absolute (global) and relative (local) extrema	177, 179–183, 194–197, 200–203, 206–213
d. Modeling rates of change, including related rates problems	232–236
e. Use of implicit differentiation to find the derivative of an inverse function	158–160, 166, 169
f. Interpretation of derivative as a rate of change in varied applied contexts, including velocity, speed, and acceleration	122–129, 136–137, 143, 160, 164–166, 187, 190–191, 198–200, 232–236, 304, 309–312, 330–337, 342–346
g. Geometric interpretation of differential equations via slope fields and the relationship between slope fields and derivatives of implicitly defined functions	304–306, 325, 343–344
h. Numerical solution of differential equations using Euler's method	350–353
i. L'Hôpital's rule and its use in determining convergence of improper integrals and series	417–423, 439
6. Computation of derivatives	
a. Knowledge of derivatives of basic functions, including x^r, exponential, trigonometric, and inverse trigonometric functions	112–113, 117–118, 134–136, 138, 153–154, 157–161, 163–169
b. Basic rules for the derivative of sums, products, and quotients of functions	113–118, 136, 534–535
c. Chain rule and implicit differentiation	141–146, 149–154, 168
d. Derivatives of parametric, polar, and vector functions	144–145, 513–514, 532–535, 559–561

C Integrals

	Pages
1. Riemann sums	
a. Concept of a Riemann sum over equal subdivisions	247–253, 260–262, 264–265, 271, 364–370, 374–375, 383, 387, 395–397, 402–404
b. Computation of Riemann sums using left, right, and midpoint evaluation points	248–253
2. Interpretations and properties of definite integrals	
a. Definite integral as a limit of Riemann sums	258–265, 271, 364–370, 374–375, 383, 387, 395–397, 402–404
b. Definite integral of the rate of change of a quantity over an interval interpreted as the change of the quantity over the interval: $$\int_{b}^{a} f'(x)dx = f(b) - f(a)$$	363–370
c. Basic properties of definite integrals	268–270
3. Applications of integrals	262–263, 265, 270–272, 283–285, 309–312, 325, 363–370, 374–379, 383–389, 395–398, 401–407, 440–441, 514–517, 536, 561–565
4. Fundamental Theorem of Calculus	
a. Use of the Fundamental Theorem to evaluate definite integrals	282–285 (and throughout from here on)
b. Use of the Fundamental Theorem to represent a particular antiderivative, and the analytical and graphical analysis of functions so defined	272–274 (exploratory), 277–282, 308, 316

	Pages
5. Techniques of antidifferentiation	
a. Antiderivatives following directly from derivatives of basic functions	190–191, 283–285, 307–309, 535–536
b. Antiderivatives by substitution of variables (including change of limits for definite integrals)	315–320
c. Antiderivatives by parts and simple partial fractions (nonrepeating linear factors only)	323–328, 444–445
d. Improper integrals (as limits of definite integrals)	433–441
6. Applications of antidifferentiation	
a. Finding specific antiderivatives using initial conditions, including applications to motion along a line	190–191, 280, 303, 309–312, 363–365, 367
b. Solving separable differential equations and using them in modeling	304–305, 320–321, 330–337, 342–346 (exponential growth in precalculus framework 20–23)
c. Solving logistic differential equations and using them in modeling	343–346
7. Numerical approximations to definite integrals	247–253, 265–266 (numerical integration using calculator occurs throughout from here on), 289–294

	Pages
1. Concept of series	457–465
2. Series of constants	
a. Motivating examples including decimal expansion	457–460
b. Geometric series with applications	459–461, 481, 488, 500, 505
c. The harmonic series	497–498
d. Alternating series with error bound	500–505
e. Terms of series as areas of rectangles and their relationship to improper integrals, including the integral test and its use in testing the convergence of p-series	492–493, 496–498, 505
f. The ratio test for convergence and divergence	491–493, 503–505
g. Comparing series to test for convergence or divergence	489–491, 498–500, 504–505
3. Taylor series	
a. Taylor polynomial approximation with graphical demonstration of convergence	469–476, 480–482, 488
b. The general Taylor series centered at $x = a$	475–476, 482
c. Maclaurin series for the functions e^x, $\sin x$, $\cos x$, and $1/(1-x)$	460–461, 465, 470–474, 476–477, 480, 482–484
d. Formal manipulation of Taylor series and shortcuts to computing Taylor series, including differentiation, antidifferentiation, and the formation of new series from known series	461–465, 476
e. Functions defined by power series and radius of convergence	460–465, 469–477, 482–484, 487–493, 503–506
f. Lagrange error bound for Taylor polynomials	482–484

AB Calculus Pacing Guide

NOTE: This timeline is based on a school year starting after Labor Day, with approximately 160 teaching days before the Advanced Placement exam.

This timeline gives approximately 15 days to "review" the course before the exam. This review time is essential and 3 weeks is a *minimum* time to set aside for this purpose.

BC Calculus Pacing Guide

Chapter 1   Prerequisites for Calculus   **4 days**

1.1 Lines   0
1.2 Functions and Graphs   0
1.3 Exponential Functions   1
1.4 Parametric Equations   1
1.5 Functions and Logarithms   1
1.6 Trigonometric Functions   1
Review Exercises/Test

Chapter 2   Limits and Continuity   **6 days**

2.1 Rates of Change and Limits   1
2.2 Limits Involving Infinity   1
2.3 Continuity   1
2.4 Rates of Change and Tangent Lines   1
Review Exercises/Test   2

Chapter 3   Derivatives   **22 days**

3.1 Derivative of a Function   2
3.2 Differentiability   2
3.3 Rules for Differentiation   2
3.4 Velocity and Other Rates of Change   2
3.5 Derivatives of Trigonometric Functions   2
3.6 Chain Rule   2
3.7 Implicit Differentiation   2
3.8 Derivatives of Inverse Trigonometric Functions   2
3.9 Derivatives of Exponential and Logarithmic Functions   3
Review Exercises/Test   3

Chapter 4   Applications of Derivatives   **14 days**

4.1 Extreme Values of Functions   2
4.2 Mean Value Theorem   1
4.3 Connecting f' and f'' with the Graph of f 2
4.4 Modeling and Optimization   3
4.5 Linearization (and Newton's Method optional)   1
4.6 Related Rates   3
Review Exercises/Test   2

Chapter 5   The Definite Integral   **16 days**

5.1 Estimating with Finite Sums   2
5.2 Definite Integrals   3
5.3 Definite Integrals and Antiderivatives   5
5.4 Fundamental Theorem of Calculus   3
5.5 Trapezoidal Rule   1
Review Exercises/Test   2

Chapter 6   Differential Equations and Mathematical Modeling   22 days

6.1 Antiderivatives and Slope Fields	3
6.2 Integration by Substitution	3
6.3 Integration by Parts	2
6.4 Exponential Growth and Decay	3
6.5 Population Growth	5
6.6 Numerical Methods	3
Review Exercises/Test	3

Chapter 7   Applications of Definite Integrals   15 days

7.1 Integral as Net Change	4
7.2 Areas in the Plane	2
7.3 Volumes	3
7.4 Lengths of Curves	2
7.5 Applications from Science and Statistics	2
Review Exercises/Test	3

Chapter 8   L'Hôpital's Rule, Improper Integrals, and Partial Fractions   7 days

8.1 L'Hôpital's Rule	1
8.2 Relative Rates of Growth	1
8.3 Improper Integrals	2
8.4 Partial Fractions and Integral Tables	1
Review Exercises/Test	2

Chapter 9   Infinite Series   23 days

9.1 Power Series	4
9.2 Taylor Series	4
9.3 Taylor's Theorem	4
9.4 Radius of Convergence	3
9.5 Testing Convergence at Endpoints	5
Review Exercises/Test	3

Chapter 10   Parametric, Vector, and Polar Functions   16 days

10.1 Parametric Equations	2
10.2 Vectors in Plane	2
10.3 Vector-valued Functions	3
10.4 Modeling Projectile Motion	2
10.5 Polar Coordinates and Polar Graphs	2
10.6 Calculus of Polar Curves	3
Review Exercises/Test	2

NOTE: This timeline is based on a school year starting after Labor Day, with approximately 160 teaching days before the Advanced Placement exam.

This timeline gives approximately 15 days to "review" the course before the exam. This review time is essential and 3 weeks is a *minimum* time to set aside for this purpose.

AB Calculus Assignment Guide

Chapter 1 — 11 days

Days	Sections	Exercises	
1	1.1	3–36 multiples of 3, 37, 39, 43, 49	
2–3	1.2	3–33 multiples of 3, 35, 36, 39, 42, 45, 49, 53, 57, 63, 65, 66	
4	1.3	3–21 multiples of 3, 22, 24–29, 34, 38	
5–6	1.4	3, 6, 7–27 odd, 30, 42	
7	1.5	3–42 multiples of 3, 43, 48, 50	
8–9	1.6	2–34 even, 38, 45	
10–11		Review and Test	

Chapter 2 — 10 days

Days	Sections	Exercises	Preparation for Advanced Placement Exam
12–13	2.1	3–30 multiples of 3, 32, 35, 39, 42, 44, 45, 48, 49, 55, 58	45–52
14–15	2.2	3–48 multiples of 3, 54, 57, 59	47, 48
16–17	2.3	2–30 even, 36, 39, 42, 48	43
18–19	2.4	1–33 odd	25, 26, 30, 32, 41
20–21		Review and Test	29, 41, 42

Chapter 3 — 30 days

Days	Sections	Exercises	Preparation for Advanced Placement Exam
22–24	3.1	1–6, 7–25 odd	21, 25, 26
25–27	3.2	1–17 odd, 18–23	29, 31
28–31	3.3	1–33 odd, 34	28, 30
32–34	3.4	1, 2, 4, 5, 10, 13, 14, 16, 24, 25, 27, 29, 30, 31, 33, 37, 38	16, 21, 23–26, 29, 36
35–37	3.5	1–10, 12–22 even, 25, 27, 29, 33	20, 27, 31
38–40	3.6	3–69 multiples of 3	50, 57, 61, 64
41–42	3.7	3–45 multiples of 3, 46, 50	40–42, 48
43–44	3.8	1–17 odd, 21, 24, 27, 30	21–23
45–48	3.9	1–41 odd, 47, 48, 50, 52	49, 53
49–51		Review and Test	59–67, 70, 78

Chapter 4 — 25 days

Days	Sections	Exercises	Preparation for Advanced Placement Exam
52–56	4.1	1–9 odd, 11–30, 37–45 odd, 48, 49, 52	35, 36, 45–49
57–58	4.2	3–33 multiples of 3, 39, 42, 43, 45, 48, 52	43
59–62	4.3	1–29 odd, 37, 40, 42–46, 48	3–6, 33, 34, 41, 42, 50
63–67	4.4	1, 5, 8, 9, 12, 17, 19, 20, 26, 31, 35, 36, 38, 40, 41, 43, 45, 46, 49, 50	41, 45–50
68–70	4.5	3, 5–9, 11, 14, 15, 18, 19, 22, 25, 27, 30, 33, 36, 39, 44, 50, 51	37, 46
71–73	4.6	3, 6, 9, 12, 13, 15, 18, 21, 22, 24–39 multiples of 3	23, 34, 39, 40
74–76		Review and Test	23, 32, 35–39, 53, 56, 58, 67

Chapter 5 — 26 days

Days	Sections	Exercises	Preparation for Advanced Placement Exam
77–79	5.1	1–4, 6, 9, 12, 14, 15, 18, 20, 21, 24, 26	24
80–83	5.2	1, 3–27 multiples of 3, 39–41, 43, 46, 47	43–46
84–91	5.3	1, 3, 4, 6, 7–17, 20, 21, 24, 25, 28, 29, 32, 36, 38, 40, 43, 44	2, 4, 29, 33–35
92–96	5.4	1–13 odd, 15–48 multiples of 3, 49, 51, 52, 54, 59, 60	53–56, 60, 64
97–99	5.5	1, 4, 6–8, 10, 11, 13, 16–18, 23	19
100–102		Review and Test	46, 51, 54

Chapter 6 — 22 days

Days	Sections	Exercises	Preparation for Advanced Placement Exam
103–106	6.1	3–24 multiples of 3, 25, 27–51 multiples of 3, 52, 61	49, 53–55, 57, 62
107–110	6.2	1–17 odd, 18–42 multiples of 3, 43, 44, 49	44, 45, 49
	6.3		
111–114	6.4	1–9 odd, 12, 14, 15–33 multiples of 3	12, 17, 25, 27, 29
115–118	6.5	1–29 odd	20, 21, 31, 32
119–121	6.6	2, 3, 6, 7, 9, 12, 15, 17, 19, 22, 24, 25, 28	16
122–124		Review and Test	33, 34, 39, 52, 54

Days	Sections	Exercises	Preparation for Advanced Placement Exam
125–129	7.1	1–17, 20–22, 24–27, 29, 31	12–16, 17, 19, 21–24
130–132	7.2	1–29 odd, 33, 36, 40, 42, 43, 46	36–38, 46
133–137	7.3	1–25 odd, 28, 29, 33, 39, 42, 44, 49, 53, 57, 60, 63	7, 12, 49–51
	7.4		
138–142	7.5	1, 3, 5, 6, 8, 10, 12, 17, 21, 24–31, 33, 35, 37, 39	25
143–145		Review and Test	2, 3, 5, 15, 17, 19, 24, 30–31, 39

BC Calculus Assignment Guide

Chapter 1 — 4 days

Days	Sections	Exercises	Preparation for Advanced Placement Exam
	1.1		
	1.2		
1	1.3	3–21 multiples of 3, 22, 24–29, 34, 38	
2	1.4	3–30 multiples of 3, 42	
3	1.5	3–42 multiples of 3, 43, 48, 50, 54	
4	1.6	3–30 multiples of 3, 32, 34, 38, 45	
		Review and Test	

Chapter 2 — 6 days

Days	Sections	Exercises	Preparation for Advanced Placement Exam
5	2.1	3–30 multiples of 3, 32, 35, 42, 44, 48, 49, 55, 58	45–52
6	2.2	3–27 multiples of 3, 37, 39, 42, 48, 54, 57, 59	47, 48
7	2.3	3–30 multiples of 3, 36, 39, 42, 48	43
8	2.4	1–25 odd, 29, 31, 33	25, 26, 30, 32, 41
9–10		Review and Test	29, 41, 42

Chapter 3 — 22 days

Days	Sections	Exercises	Preparation for Advanced Placement Exam
11–12	3.1	1–15 odd, 16, 17–25 odd	21, 25, 26
13–14	3.2	1–23 odd, 30, 31	29, 31
15–16	3.3	1–33 odd, 34	28, 30
17–18	3.4	1, 2, 4, 5, 10, 13, 14, 16, 24, 25, 27, 29, 30, 31, 33, 37, 38	16, 21, 23–26, 29, 36
19–20	3.5	2–22 even, 25, 27, 29, 33	20, 27, 31
21–22	3.6	3–69 multiples of 3	50, 57, 61, 64
23–24	3.7	3–42 multiples of 3, 43, 45, 46, 50	40–42, 48
25–26	3.8	3–18 multiples of 3, 19, 21–33 multiples of 3	21–23
27–29	3.9	3–42 multiples of 3, 47, 48, 50, 52	49, 53
30–32		Review and Test	59–67, 70, 78

Chapter 4 — 14 days

Days	Sections	Exercises	Preparation for Advanced Placement Exam
33–34	4.1	1–9 odd, 12–30 multiples of 3, 37, 39, 42, 45, 48, 49, 52	35, 36, 45–49
35	4.2	3–33 multiples of 3, 39, 43, 45, 48, 52	43
36–37	4.3	1–11 odd, 15–30 multiples of 3, 37, 40, 42, 44, 48	3–6, 33, 34, 41, 42, 50
38–40	4.4	1, 5, 9, 12, 17, 19, 20, 26, 31, 35, 36, 38, 40, 41, 43, 45, 46, 49, 50	41, 45–50
41–42	4.5	3, 5–9, 11, 14, 15, 18, 19, 22, 25, 27, 30, 33, 36, 39, 44, 50, 51	37, 46
43–44	4.6	3, 6, 9, 12, 13, 15–39 multiples of 3	23, 34, 39, 40
45–46		Review and Test	23, 32, 35–39, 53, 56, 58, 67

Chapter 5 — 16 days

Days	Sections	Exercises	Preparation for Advanced Placement Exam
47–48	5.1	1–4, 6, 9, 12, 14, 15, 18, 20, 21, 24, 26	24
49–51	5.2	3–27 multiples of 3, 39–41, 43, 46, 47	43–46
52–56	5.3	1, 3, 4, 6, 7–17, 20, 21, 24, 25, 28, 29, 32, 36, 38, 40, 43, 44	2, 4, 29, 33–35
57–59	5.4	1–13 odd, 15–51 multiples of 3, 52, 54, 59	53–56, 60, 64
60	5.5	1, 4, 7, 8, 10, 11, 13, 16–18, 23	19
61–62		Review and Test	46, 51, 54

Chapter 6 — 22 days

Days	Sections	Exercises	Preparation for Advanced Placement Exam
63–65	6.1	3–51 multiples of 3, 52, 61, 67	49, 53–55, 57, 62
66–68	6.2	1–17 odd, 18–42 multiples of 3, 43, 44, 49	44–45, 49
69–70	6.3	3–24 multiples of 3, 26, 27, 30, 33	23–25
71–73	6.4	1–9 odd, 12, 14, 15–33 multiples of 3	12, 17, 25, 27, 29
74–78	6.5	1–29 odd	9–12, 16, 18, 20–21
79–81	6.6	2, 3, 6, 7, 9, 12, 15, 17, 19, 22–25, 28–30	16
82–84		Review and Test	33–34, 39, 52, 54

Chapter 7 — 15 days

Days	Sections	Exercises	Preparation for Advanced Placement Exam
85–87	7.1	1–11 odd, 12–17, 20–22, 24–31	12–16, 17, 19, 21–24
88	7.2	3–33 multiples of 3, 35, 40, 42, 43, 46	36–38, 43, 46
89–91	7.3	1–17 odd, 22, 25, 28, 29, 33, 39, 42, 44, 49, 53, 57, 60, 63	7, 12, 49–50
92–93	7.4	3–21 multiples of 3, 22–24, 27, 30	19, 21, 25, 27, 29
94–96	7.5	3, 5, 6, 9, 12, 17, 21, 25–31, 33, 35, 37	25
97–99		Review and Test	2–3, 5, 15, 17, 19, 24, 30–31, 39

Chapter 8 — 7 days

Days	Sections	Exercises	Preparation for Advanced Placement Exam
100	8.1	3, 6, 9, 12, 15–45 odd, 48, 50, 52	47, 48, 51
101	8.2	3–36 multiples of 3, 37, 40, 42, 43	37, 38
102–103	8.3	3–48 multiples of 3, 49, 51, 52, 55, 56	49, 52–53
104	8.4	3–42 multiples of 3, 43–48 29–30	4, 47
105–106		Review and Test	27, 61, 67–69

Chapter 9 — 23 days

Days	Sections	Exercises	Preparation for Advanced Placement Exam
107–110	9.1	1–10, 11–23 odd, 26–28, 32, 34, 36–38, 42, 45, 48, 51, 52, 54, 55	20, 25, 38, 47, 50–52
111–114	9.2	1–31 odd	16–22, 29–31
115–118	9.3	1–15 odd, 16, 18, 20, 23–25, 28, 29	12, 15, 21, 24–26, 27
119–121	9.4	3–39 multiples of 3, 45, 48, 51	38, 40, 50, 52
122–126	9.5	1–41 odd, 44–47, 49–55 odd	46, 48–52, 54
127–129		Review and Test	56–61, 63

Chapter 10 — 16 days

Days	Sections	Exercises	Preparation for Advanced Placement Exam
130–131	10.1	1–31 odd, 32, 33	16, 27, 31
132–133	10.2	3–24 multiples of 3, 35, 37, 39, 40, 43, 44, 47, 50	24
134–136	10.3	1–27 odd, 31, 35, 38	13, 16, 18, 21, 24, 29, 31, 33–34
137–138	10.4	1, 3, 5–7, 9–17 odd, 18, 21, 26–28	13, 18–19
139–140	10.5	1, 3, 5, 6–57 multiples of 3, 65	68
141–143	10.6	1–7 odd, 13–27 odd, 30–42 even, 45	25, 28, 44
144–145		Review and Test	13, 46, 53, 58, 61, 63

1.2–1.6 Concepts Worksheet

Graphical Analysis

Chapter 1 deals with functions and their graphical characteristics. To facilitate a study of functions, it is important to visualize mentally the graph of a function when given an algebraic description.

1. Graph each function. Clearly indicate units on the axes provided.

(a) $f(x) = x^2$

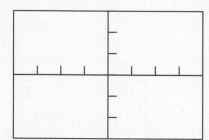

(b) $f(x) = x^3$

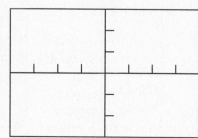

(c) $f(x) = |x|$

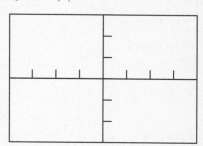

(d) $f(x) = \sin x$

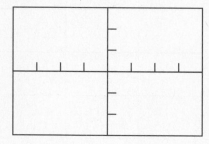

(e) $f(x) = \cos x$

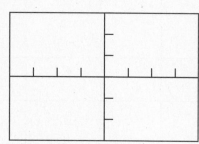

(f) $f(x) = \tan x$

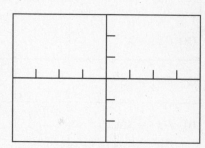

(g) $f(x) = \sec x$

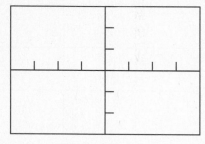

(h) $f(x) = 2^x$

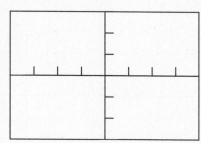

(i) $f(x) = \log_2 x$

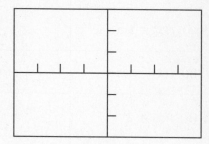

(j) $f(x) = \dfrac{1}{x}$

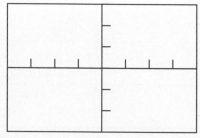

(k) $f(x) = \sqrt{x}$

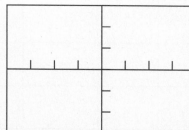

(l) $f(x) = \sqrt{a^2 - x^2}$

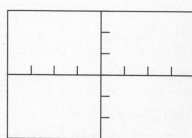

Continued

2. Answer the following questions about the indicated functions. In completing the table below, you may use the following abbreviations, *R*: the set of real numbers, *J*: the set of integers, and *N*: the set of natural numbers. Note: This exercise may need to be done as appropriate sections of Chapter 1 are completed.

Function	Domain	Range $y = f(x)$	Zeros (Find x when $f(x) = 0$)	Symmetry with respect to y-axis or origin	Even or Odd Function— $f(-x) = f(x)$ or $f(-x) = -f(x)$	Is the function periodic? If so, state the period.	Is $f(x)$ a one-to-one function? (For each $f(x)$ only one x exists)
(a) $f(x) = x^2$							
(b) $f(x) = x^3$							
(c) $f(x) = |x|$							
(d) $f(x) = \sin x$							
(e) $f(x) = \cos x$							
(f) $f(x) = \tan x$							
(g) $f(x) = \sec x$							
(h) $f(x) = 2^x$							
(i) $f(x) = \log_2 x$							
(j) $f(x) = \dfrac{1}{x}$							
(k) $f(x) = \sqrt{x}$							
(l) $f(x) = \sqrt{a^2 - x^2}$							

Concept Connectors

3. Is there a relationship between symmetry in a function's graph and the function's being even or odd? Explain.

_____

_____

_____

4. Draw a reflection of **(a)** $f(x) = \sin x$, **(b)** $f(x) = 2^x$ and **(c)** $f(x) = \sqrt{x}$ through the *x*-axis.

(a)

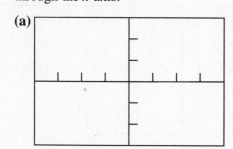

(b)

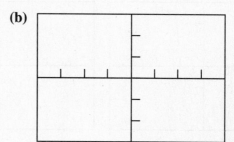

(c)

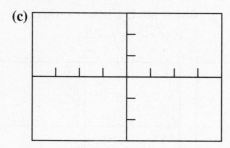

5. Draw a reflection of **(a)** $f(x) = \sin x$, **(b)** $f(x) = 2^x$ and **(c)** $f(x) = \sqrt{x}$ through the *y*-axis.

(a)

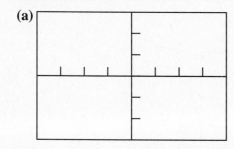

(b)

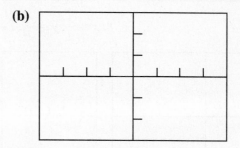

(c)

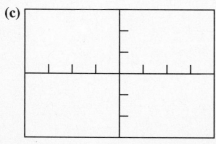

1.4 Concepts Worksheet

Parametric Equations

The mention of the curve $y = x^2$ should summon an immediate mental image of a parabola on the coordinate plane. The following parametric curve descriptions are related to the curve $y = x^2$, but perhaps do not evoke a mental image as quickly. Graph the following curves indicating direction for increasing values of t in the domain of each curve. Also indicate the value(s) of t corresponding to the domain endpoints and the point corresponding to $t = 0$, if any.

1. $x = t, y = t^2$

2. $x = -t, y = t^2$

3. $x = t^2, y = t$

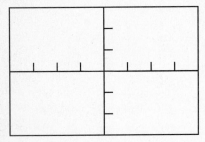

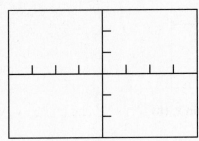

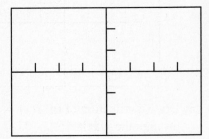

4. $x = t^2, y = t^4$

5. $x = \sin t, y = 1 - \cos^2 t$

6. $x = \sec t, y = \sec^2 t$ where $0 \le t \le \pi, t \ne \dfrac{\pi}{2}$

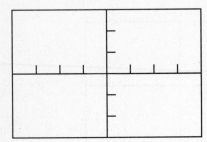

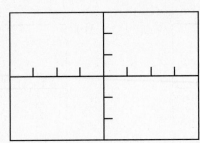

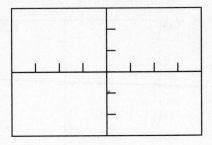

7. $x = e^t, y = e^{2t}$

8. $x = \dfrac{1}{t}, y = \dfrac{1}{t^2}, t \ne 0$

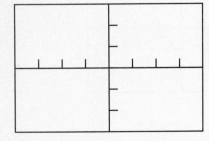

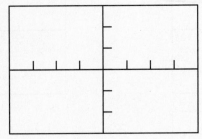

1.4 Concepts Worksheet

NAME

Continued

9. In parametric form a graph can easily be reflected over the line $y = x$. If the graph of $x = f(t)$, $y = g(t)$ is reflected over the line $y = x$, the new graph is described by $x = $ _____, $y = $ _____. Which of the above curves (1–8) is a reflection over the line $y = x$ of the graph of $y = x^2$? _____

10. For Exercise 7, find a corresponding parametric description of the reflection of the curve over the line $y = x$, then sketch the graph.

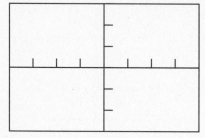

11. The following graphs of $y^2 = x$ or $y = \sqrt{x}$ are drawn indicating direction for increasing values of t. Provide a parametric description of each:

(a)
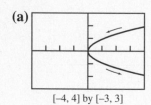
[–4, 4] by [–3, 3]

_____

(b)
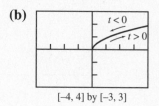
[–4, 4] by [–3, 3]

_____

© Addison Wesley Longman, Inc.

Calculus Concepts Worksheets **25**

2.2–2.3 Concepts Worksheet

End Behavior Models

For each pair of graphs shown, determine whether $g(x)$ appears to be a right end behavior model for $f(x)$, a left end behavior model for $f(x)$, both, or neither.

1. $y = f(x)$

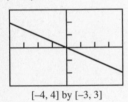

[−4, 4] by [−3, 3]

$y = g(x)$

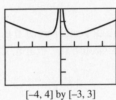

[−4, 4] by [−3, 3]

_____

2. $y = f(x)$

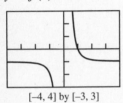

[−4, 4] by [−3, 3]

$y = g(x)$

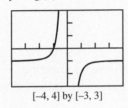

[−4, 4] by [−3, 3]

_____

3. $y = f(x)$

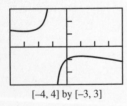

[−4, 4] by [−3, 3]

$y = g(x)$

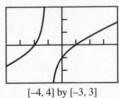

[−4, 4] by [−3, 3]

_____

4. $y = f(x)$

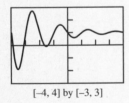

[−4, 4] by [−3, 3]

$y = g(x)$

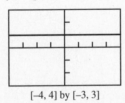

[−4, 4] by [−3, 3]

_____

Continuity

5. Decide whether the functions represented by the following graphs
are continuous at $x = c$. If the function is discontinuous at c, identify
the type of discontinuity.

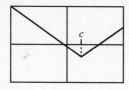

(a) _____

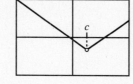

(b) _____

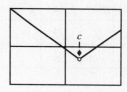

(c) _____

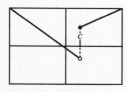

(d) _____

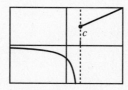

(e) _____

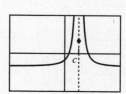

(f) _____

6. Give an example of a function that has:

(a) only one point of discontinuity   _____

(b) exactly two points of discontinuity   _____

(c) an infinite number of points of discontinuity   _____

7. Give an example of a function that is:

(a) continuous at every point   _____

(b) discontinuous at every point   _____

3.1–3.3 Concepts Worksheet

Differentiation

1. Given the following information about differentiable functions $f(x)$ and $g(x)$ at $x = 2$ and $x = 3$,

x	$f(x)$	$g(x)$	$f'(x)$	$g'(x)$
2	8	2	1/3	−3
3	3	−4	2π	5

determine the value of:

_____ a) $\dfrac{d}{dx}\{2f(x)\}$ at $x = 2$

_____ b) $\dfrac{d}{dx}\{f(x) + g(x)\}$ at $x = 3$

_____ c) $\dfrac{d}{dx}\{f(x) \cdot g(x)\}$ at $x = 3$

_____ d) $\dfrac{d}{dx}\left\{\dfrac{f(x)}{g(x)}\right\}$ at $x = 2$

_____ e) $\dfrac{d}{dx}\{f(g(x))\}$ at $x = 2$

_____ f) $\dfrac{d}{dx}\{\sqrt{f(x)}\}$ at $x = 2$

_____ g) $\dfrac{d}{dx}\left\{\dfrac{1}{g(x)}\right\}$ at $x = 3$

_____ h) If $h(x) = \sqrt{f^2(x) + g^2(x)}$, then find $h'(2)$.

2.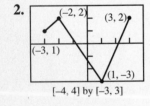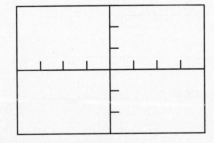

The graph of $f(x)$ with domain $[-3, 3]$ is composed of line segments as shown above.

(a) Sketch the graph of $f'(x)$ on the grid above.

(b) Name the x-coordinate of each point of discontinuity of $f'(x)$ over $(-3, 3)$.

_____

Continued

Concept Connectors

3. What points do you suspect of being points of discontinuity of the derivatives of these graphs? (Give the x-coordinates of the points of discontinuity of $f'(x)$.)

(a) $f(x) = x^2$ **(b)** $f(x) = |x| - 1$ **(c)** $f(x) = x^{1/3}$

_____   _____   _____

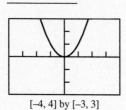
[−4, 4] by [−3, 3]

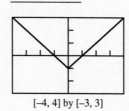
[−4, 4] by [−3, 3]

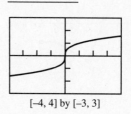
[−4, 4] by [−3, 3]

(d) $f(x) = x^{2/3}$ **(e)** $f(x) = |\ln x|$ **(f)** $f(x) = 2 \sin \dfrac{6}{x}$

_____   _____   _____

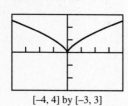
[−4, 4] by [−3, 3]

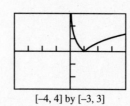
[−4, 4] by [−3, 3]

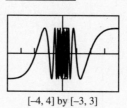
[−4, 4] by [−3, 3]

4. You may not have *formally* arrived at the "suspect" points called for above. Formal limit computations as described in Appendix A3 would rigorously prove derivative discontinuities. However, some of the examples used above would still seem difficult. In general, which characteristics on a curve would make you believe that the slope of a tangent line to the curve at that point is nonexistent?

_____

_____

3.4 Concepts Worksheet

Velocity, Speed, and Acceleration

1. The graph shows the position $s(t)$ of a particle moving along a
   horizontal coordinate axis.

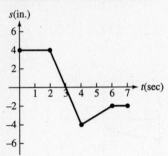

(a) When is the particle moving to the left? _____

(b) When is the particle moving to the right? _____

(c) When is the particle standing still? _____

(d) Graph the particle's velocity and speed (where defined).

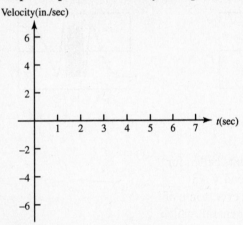

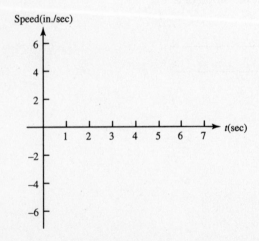

(e) When is the particle moving fastest? _____

Continued

2. The graph shows the velocity $v = f(t)$ of a particle moving along a horizontal coordinate axis.

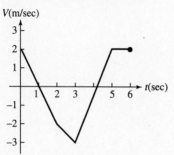

(a) When does the particle reverse direction? _____

(b) When is the particle moving at a constant speed? _____

(c) When is the particle moving at its greatest speed? _____

(d) Graph the acceleration (where defined).

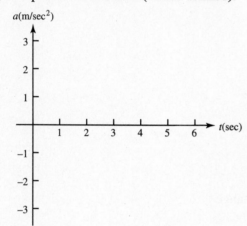

3. A particle moves along a vertical coordinate axis so that its position at any time $t \geq 0$ is given by the function $s(t) = \frac{1}{3}t^3 - 3t^2 + 8t - 4$, where s is measured in centimeters and t is measured in seconds.

(a) Find the displacement during the first 6 seconds.

_____

(b) Find the average velocity during the first 6 seconds.

_____

(c) Find expressions for the velocity and acceleration at time t.
   $v(t) =$ _____ $a(t) =$ _____

(d) For what values of t is the particle moving downward?

_____

4. The values of the coordinate *s* of a moving body for various values of *t* are given below.

t(sec)	0	0.5	1.0	1.5	2.0	2.5	3.0	3.5	4.0
s(ft)	40.0	35.0	30.2	36.0	48.2	45.0	38.2	16.0	0.2

(a) Plot *s* versus *t*, and sketch a smooth curve through the given points.

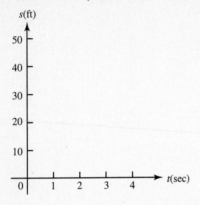

(b) Estimate the velocity at each of the following times.
At *t* = 0.5 sec, *v* ≈ _____ .
At *t* = 2.5 sec, *v* ≈ _____ .
At *t* = 3 sec, *v* ≈ _____ .

(c) At what approximate values of *t* does the particle change direction?

_____

(d) At what approximate value of *t* is the particle moving at the greatest speed?

_____

Continued

Concept Connector

5. The position (*x*-coordinate) of a particle moving on the horizontal line $x = 1$ is given by $x(t) = t^3 - 15t^2 + 63t - 45$ for $t \geq 0$.

   (a) Use analytic methods to determine when the particle changes its direction of motion and its position at each of these times.
   At $t =$ _____, $x =$ _____.
   At $t =$ _____, $x =$ _____.

   Now graph the parametric equations
   $x(t) = t^3 - 15t^2 + 63t - 45$, $y(t) = 1$, in a
   $[-50, 50]$ by $[-1, 2.1]$ viewing window for $0 \leq t \leq 10$. Use TRACE to confirm the results you found analytically.

   (b) When graphing parametric equations for horizontal motion on a graphing calculator, you can see the motion better if you let the *y*-coordinate increase slightly every time the particle changes direction. Instead of $y(t) = 1$, let
   $y(t) = 1 + 0.1(t \geq A) + 0.1(t \geq B)$, where *A* and *B* are the *t*-values you found in part (a). Sketch the resulting graph below.

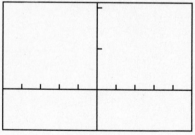

   $[-50, 50]$ by $[-1, 2.1]$

3.7 Concepts Worksheet

Implicit Differentiation

Let $y = f(x)$ be the continuous function satisfying the equation
$x^5 + x^4y - xy^2 - y^3 = 0$ and containing the points $\left(-\frac{1}{2}, \frac{1}{2}\right)$, $(-2, 2)$,
and $(2, 4)$.

1. Find an expression for $\dfrac{dy}{dx}$ in terms of x and y.

2. Find $\dfrac{dy}{dx}$ at each of the following points.

   (a) $\left(-\dfrac{1}{2}, \dfrac{1}{2}\right)$ _____ **(b)** $(-2, 2)$ _____ **(c)** $(2, 4)$ _____

3. Note that $x^5 + x^4y - xy^2 - y^3 = (x + y)(x^2 + y)(x^2 - y) = 0$. Use this factorization to graph the function $y = f(x)$, described earlier.

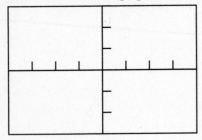

4. Can the expression you wrote in question 1 above be used to find $\dfrac{dy}{dx}$ at $(0, 0)$? Explain.

   _____

   _____

5. Evaluate $\lim\limits_{x \to 0^+} \dfrac{f(x) - f(0)}{x - 0}$. _____

6. Evaluate $\lim\limits_{x \to 0^-} \dfrac{f(x) - f(0)}{x - 0}$. _____

7. Can you evaluate $f'(0)$? _____ Why or why not? _____

   _____

Continued

Concept Connectors

We have yet to discuss the calculus of exponential and logarithmic functions. However, a sense of their differentiation could be developed geometrically:

Note the following graphs of exponential functions.

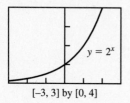

[–3, 3] by [0, 4]

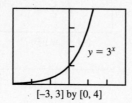

[–3, 3] by [0, 4]

Imagine a sketch of the "derivative" graphs on the curves above. Since precise range values of the derivative are still open to interpretation using this technique, it may appear that the derivative graphs for 2^x and 3^x are much like the curves themselves. In fact, the derivative of 2^x is the product of 2^x and some positive constant $c = 0.693$, which is less than 1, while the derivative 3^x is the product of 3^x and some positive constant $d = 1.09$, which is greater than 1.

8. Hence, one might conclude that there exists an exponential function whose derivative is itself, and that the base of this exponential function lies between _____ and _____.

9. Surely, a beautiful curve in the calculus would be one whose derivative curve is itself. Cite an example, previously studied, of a function whose derivative is itself. _____

3.8 Concepts Worksheet

Inverse Functions

Given the graph $f(x)$, roughly sketch $f^{-1}(x)$ on the same grid.

1.
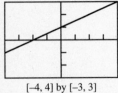
[–4, 4] by [–3, 3]

2.
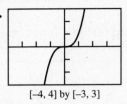
[–4, 4] by [–3, 3]

3.
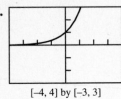
[–4, 4] by [–3, 3]

4.
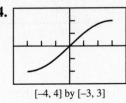
[–4, 4] by [–3, 3]

5. Which of the following have inverse functions?

a.
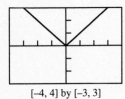
[–4, 4] by [–3, 3]

b.
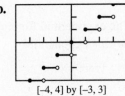
[–4, 4] by [–3, 3]

c.
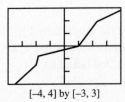
[–4, 4] by [–3, 3]

d.
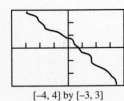
[–4, 4] by [–3, 3]

e.
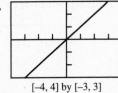
[–4, 4] by [–3, 3]

f.
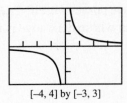
[–4, 4] by [–3, 3]

6. Which of the functions in Problem 5 appear to have an inverse function whose graph is the same as the original graph?

Continued

Concept Connectors

7. If $f(g(x)) = g(f(x)) = x$, what is the relationship between functions f and g? _____

8. Use implicit differentiation to find an expression for $g'(x)$ using $f(g(x)) = x$, assuming both f and g are differentiable.

_____

Let f be a differentiable function with the $f(x)$ and $f'(x)$ values given in the table below. Assume that f has a differentiable inverse function, $g(x) = f^{-1}(x)$.

x	$f(x)$	$f'(x)$
1	-3	4
2	1	5
3	2	6

9. Complete the table to give as much information as possible about the inverse function.

x	$g(x)$	$g'(x)$

10. Find an equation of the line tangent to the graph of $y = f(x)$ at $x = 1$.

_____

11. Find an equation of the line tangent to the graph of $y = g(x)$ at $x = 1$.

_____

12. Find an equation of the line normal to the graph of $y = g(x)$ at $x = 2$.

_____

3.9 Concepts Worksheet

Why "e"?

You have learned that e is a special number in part because the derivative of e^x is e^x itself. To establish more firmly the constants involved in the differentiation of exponential functions, let us use the definition of the derivative to calculate the derivatives of $f(x) = 2^x$ and $g(x) = 3^x$.

1. If $f(x) = 2^x$ Similarly, complete the following.

$$f'(x) = \lim_{h \to 0} \frac{2^{x+h} - 2^x}{h} \qquad\qquad g'(x) = \underline{\hspace{4cm}}$$

$$= \lim_{h \to 0} \frac{2^x \cdot 2^h - 2^x}{h} \qquad\qquad = \underline{\hspace{4cm}}$$

$$= \lim_{h \to 0} \frac{2^x(2^h - 1)}{h} \qquad\qquad = \underline{\hspace{4cm}}$$

$$= 2^x \cdot \lim_{h \to 0} \frac{2^h - 1}{h} \qquad\qquad = 3^x \cdot \lim_{h \to 0} \frac{3^h - 1}{h}$$

$\underbrace{\hspace{3cm}}$ $\underbrace{\hspace{3cm}}$

This is a "mysterious" constant of differentiation.   This is a "mysterious" constant of differentiation

2. To help resolve the "mystery" of the above limits, generate the following values using a calculator:

h	1	-1	0.1	-0.1	0.01	-0.01	0.001	-0.001	0.0001	-0.0001
$\dfrac{2^h - 1}{h}$										
$\dfrac{3^h - 1}{h}$										

3. It appears that the limits exist and that an approximation to the thousandths place is:

$$\lim_{h \to 0} \frac{2^h - 1}{h} \approx \underline{\hspace{5cm}}$$

$$\lim_{h \to 0} \frac{3^h - 1}{h} \approx \underline{\hspace{5cm}}$$

Continued

Would it not be "nice" to find an exponential function whose constant of differentiation is 1? You should now strongly suspect that the base of such an exponential function lies between 2 and 3, and so, perhaps, an iterative search on your calculator would further define the number. For example,

$$\lim_{h \to 0} \frac{(2.5)^h - 1}{h} < 1$$

while

$$\lim_{h \to 0} \frac{(2.75)^h - 1}{h} > 1, \text{ and so on.}$$

Though this search may seem tedious, it should help you to further appreciate this "nice" irrational number that is called "e" ($e = 2.718\ldots$) and the exponential function $f(x) = e^x$ whose derivative is itself.

Concept Connectors

Every exponential function can be expressed in terms of base e. That is ,
$a^x = (e^{\ln a})^x = e^{x \ln a}$ for $a > 0$.

4. If $f(x) = 2^x = $ _____ (express in base e),

    then $f'(x) = $ _____ . (Use the Chain Rule.)

    Therefore,

    $$\lim_{h \to 0} \frac{2^h - 1}{h} = $$ _____ . (Express in terms of ln.)

5. If $g(x) = 3^x = $ _____ (express in base e),

    then $g'(x) = $ _____ . (Use the Chain Rule.)

    Therefore,

    $$\lim_{h \to 0} \frac{3^h - 1}{h} = $$ _____ . (Express in terms of ln.)

6. We cannot classify the following function as either a polynomial or an exponential function; it seems to be a strange mix of both. However, procedures established above will lead to a derivative:

    If $h(x) = x^x = $ _____ (express in base e),

    then $h'(x) = $ _____ .

4.1 Concepts Worksheet

An Unusual Function

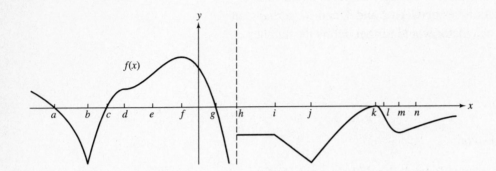

1. The function f drawn above would be difficult to describe algebraically; nevertheless, it has interesting geometric features for which calculus provides descriptions. Using the textbook definitions and some freedom of artistic judgment, name the value(s) of x for:

   (a) zeros of $f(x)$ _____

   (b) points of discontinuity of f _____

   (c) critical points _____

   (d) intervals over which f increases _____

   (e) intervals over which f decreases _____

   (f) relative maxima _____

   (g) absolute maxima _____

   (h) relative minima _____

   (i) absolute minima _____

   (j) intervals over which f is concave up _____

   (k) intervals over which f is concave down _____

   (l) points of inflection _____

2. **(a)** Find the equation of any horizontal asymptotes

   _____

   (b) Find the equation of any vertical asymptote(s)

   _____

3. Find the x-coordinate of each point of discontinuity of f'. _____

4. Find the x-coordinate of each critical point of f'. _____

5. Sketch f' on the same graph as f. (You will need to approximate the range extent of $f'(x)$ as you graph.)

4.2 Concepts Worksheet

Theorems of Calculus

Rolle's Theorem states: If a function is continuous at every point on a closed interval $[a, b]$ and differentiable on every point of its interior (a, b) and $f(a) = f(b) = 0$, then there is at least one number c between a and b at which $f'(c) = 0$.

     A variation of Rolle's Theorem includes broader conditions: If function $f(x)$ is continuous at every point in a closed interval $[a, b]$ and $f(a) = f(b)$, then there exists at least one critical point of $f(x)$ between $x = a$ and $x = b$.

1. Using this variation of Rolle's Theorem, find and mark the critical points on the following graphs, if applicable. If not applicable, explain why not.

(a)

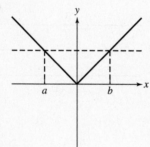

(b)

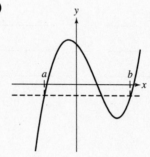

(c)

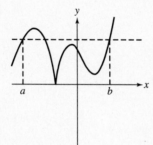

(d)

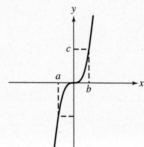

Continued

2. Given the functions below as drawn over the interval $[a, b]$, are the conditions of the Mean Value Theorem met? (If not, why not?) If conditions are met, locate the value(s) of c that satisfy the equation $f'(c) = \dfrac{f(b) - f(a)}{b - a}$. Draw the parallel tangent lines and secant line implied in the Mean Value Theorem.

(a)

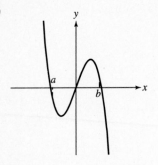

_____

_____

_____

(b)

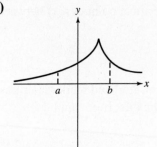

_____

_____

_____

(c)

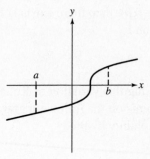

_____

_____

_____

(d)

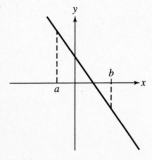

_____

_____

_____

(e)

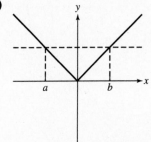

_____

_____

_____

4.2 Concepts Worksheet

NAME ______________________________

Concept Connectors

3. Suppose that $f(x)$ is a function with continuous first and second derivatives on the closed interval $[1, 3]$ whose values for f and f' at $x = 1$ and $x = 3$ are given below:

x	$f(x)$	$f'(x)$
1	5	2
3	7	−1

(a) Prove there exists a value of c, $1 < c < 3$, such that $f'(c) = 1$.

____

____

____

(b) Prove there exists a value of d, $1 < d < 3$, such that $f''(d) = -\frac{3}{2}$.

____

____

____

4.3 Concepts Worksheet

Graph Sketching Using Derivatives

1. Sketch a graph of a differentiable function $f(x)$ over the closed interval $[-2, 7]$, where $f(-2) = f(7) = -3$ and $f(4) = 3$. The roots of $f(x) = 0$ occur at $x = 0$ and $x = 6$, and $f(x)$ has properties indicated in the table below:

x	$-2 < x < 0$	$x = 0$	$0 < x < 2$	$x = 2$	$2 < x < 4$	$x = 4$	$4 < x < 7$
$f'(x)$	positive	0	positive	1	positive	0	negative
$f''(x)$	negative	0	positive	0	negative	0	negative

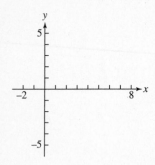

2. Sketch a graph of the continuous even function $g(x)$ over the closed interval of x values $[-5, 5]$ having a range of $g(x)$ values $[-1, 0]$. For $x \geq 0$, roots of $g(x) = 0$ occur at every whole number k and roots of $g'(x) = 0$ occur at $\frac{k}{2}$. The first and second derivatives of $g(x)$ exist everywhere except at $x = k$. Furthermore, $g''(x) > 0$ for every $x \neq k$.

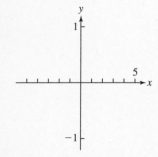

3. Sketch a function $h(x)$ from the following information:

   (a) $h(-x) = -h(x)$

   (b) $\lim\limits_{x \to 0^+} h(x) = \infty$

   (c) $\lim\limits_{x \to +\infty} h(x) = 0$

   (d) For $x > 0$, $h(x) = 0$ only at $x = 1$

   (e) For $x > 0$, $h'(x) = 0$ only at $x = 2$

   (f) For $x > 0$, $h''(x) = 0$ only at $x = 3$

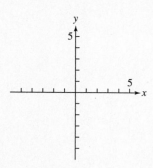

Concept Connectors

4. The graph of $f(x)$ is shown on the closed interval $[-6a, 6a]$:

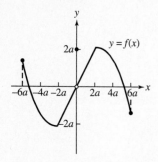

Answer the following questions regarding $f(x)$:

   (a) For $x \neq 0$, the graph of $f(x)$ has symmetry about the _____, that is $f(-x) =$ _____.

   (b) f has point(s) of discontinuity at $x =$ _____.

   (c) $\lim\limits_{x \to 0} f(x) =$ _____.

   (d) The zeros of $f(x)$ occur at $x =$ _____.

   (e) $f'(x)$ does not exist at $x =$ _____.

   (f) $f''(x) < 0$ for the x interval(s) _____.

5.2 Concepts Worksheet

Riemann Sum as a Definite Integral

Certain infinite series can be summed because they are identifiable as the Riemann sum of a definite integral. The following are all Riemann sums. The first example outlines steps in the process of converting a Riemann sum to a definite integral.

Example A:

Find a definite integral whose value is equal to

$$\lim_{n \to \infty} \left(\frac{\sqrt{1} + \sqrt{2} + \cdots + \sqrt{n}}{\sqrt{n^3}} \right).$$

Step 1: Factor out a "candidate" dx. In general, dx will be a constant divided by n. Note in this case we may use $dx = \frac{1}{n}$.

$$\lim_{n \to \infty} \left(\frac{\sqrt{1} + \sqrt{2} + \cdots + \sqrt{n}}{\sqrt{n^3}} \right) = \lim_{n \to \infty} \left(\frac{\sqrt{1} + \sqrt{2} + \cdots + \sqrt{n}}{\sqrt{n}} \right) \cdot \frac{1}{n}$$

$$= \lim_{n \to \infty} \left[\sqrt{\frac{1}{n}} + \sqrt{\frac{2}{n}} + \cdots + \sqrt{\frac{n}{n}} \right] \cdot \frac{1}{n}$$

Step 2: Identify the variable, x, by searching the summation for changing values where the absolute value of the common difference between consecutive values is dx. (There may be several possible appropriate choices for x and dx.)

x-values: $\frac{1}{n}, \frac{2}{n}, \cdots, \frac{n}{n}$ $\qquad \left(x = \frac{k}{n} \right)$

Step 3: Find the range of x values as n approaches infinity.

Limit of x-values: $\lim_{n \to \infty} \frac{1}{n} = 0$; $\lim_{n \to \infty} \frac{n}{n} = 1$

Step 4: Verify that dx is a correct "candidate" for this Riemann Sum. Specifically, dx should equal the quotient determined by the width of the range of x-values divided by the number of terms in the summation.

That is, $dx = \frac{1 - 0}{n}$, which agrees with the dx selected in Step 1.

Step 5: Identify $f(x)$, the functional operation on the x-values. Since the summation terms $\sqrt{\frac{1}{n}}, \sqrt{\frac{2}{n}}, \cdots, \sqrt{\frac{n}{n}}$ are the square roots of the x-values $\frac{1}{n}, \frac{2}{n}, \cdots, \frac{n}{n}$, we let $f(x) = \sqrt{x}$.

In summary, $\lim_{n \to \infty} \sum_{k=1}^{n} \left[\left(\sqrt{\frac{k}{n}} \right) \frac{1}{n} \right]$ is a Riemann sum, which can be expressed as $\int_{0}^{1} \sqrt{x}\, dx$, a definite integral.

Continued

Example B:

Briefly outlined:

$$\lim_{n\to\infty} \sum_{k=1}^{2n} \frac{k^3}{n^4} = \lim_{n\to\infty} \sum_{k=1}^{2n} \left[\frac{k^3}{n^3} \cdot \frac{1}{n} \right]$$

$$= \lim_{n\to\infty} \sum_{k=1}^{2n} \left[\left(\frac{k}{n}\right)^3 \cdot \frac{1}{n} \right]$$

Step 1: $dx = \dfrac{1}{n}$

Step 2: x-values: $\dfrac{1}{n}, \dfrac{2}{n}, \dfrac{3}{n}, \cdots, \dfrac{2n}{n} \qquad \left(x = \dfrac{k}{n} \right)$

Step 3: Limit of x-values: $\lim_{n\to\infty} \dfrac{1}{n} = 0; \ \lim_{n\to\infty} \dfrac{2n}{n} = 2$

Step 4: $dx = \dfrac{2-0}{2n} = \dfrac{1}{n}$, which agrees with dx chosen in Step 1.

Step 5: $f(x) = x^3$

Therefore $\lim_{n\to\infty} \sum_{k=1}^{2n} \dfrac{k^3}{n^4} = \displaystyle\int_0^2 x^3 \, dx$

Express the following Riemann Sums as definite integrals:

1. $\lim_{n\to\infty} \left[\dfrac{1}{n^3} + \dfrac{4}{n^3} + \dfrac{9}{n^3} \cdots + \dfrac{n^2}{n^3} \right]$

2. $\lim_{n\to\infty} \sum_{k=1}^{n} \left[\dfrac{k}{n} + \left(\dfrac{k}{n}\right)^2 \right] \dfrac{1}{n}$

3. $\lim_{n\to\infty} \sum_{k=1}^{n} \sqrt{\dfrac{1}{n^2}\left(1 + \dfrac{2k}{n}\right)}$

4. $\lim_{n\to\infty} \sum_{k=n+1}^{2n} \dfrac{1}{2k}$

5. $\lim_{n\to\infty} \sum_{k=1}^{2n} \left[\dfrac{1}{1 + \dfrac{2k}{n}} \cdot \dfrac{1}{n} \right]$

Continued

Concept Connectors

Based on problem 5 above, use the following choices for *x*-values and define an appropriate definite integral.

6. $x = \dfrac{k}{n}$

_____

7. $x = \dfrac{2k}{n}$

_____

8. $x = 1 + \dfrac{2k}{n}$

_____

9. Do the integrals you wrote in problems 6–8 all have the same value? Explain.

_____

_____

5.3–5.4 Concepts Worksheet

Graphical Antidifferentiation

Each of the following graphs represents the derivative of a continuous function *f*. Sketch a possible graph of $y = f(x)$ on the same set of axes as the derivative, assuming $f(0) = 0$.

1.

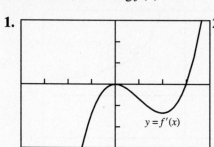

[–4, 4] by [–3, 3]

2.

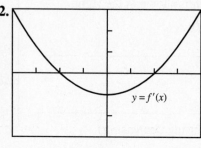

[–4, 4] by [–3, 3]

3.

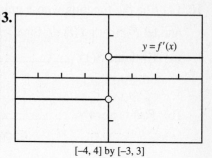

[–4, 4] by [–3, 3]

4.

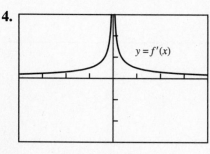

[–4, 4] by [–3, 3]

5.

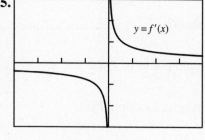

[–4, 4] by [–3, 3]

The following graphs of $f'(x)$ involve nonexistent derivatives at $x = 0$, because $f(x)$ is discontinuous at $x = 0$. Match each graph of $f(x)$ to the corresponding $f'(x)$ graph.

6.

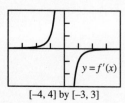

[–4, 4] by [–3, 3]

7.

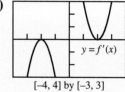

[–4, 4] by [–3, 3]

8.

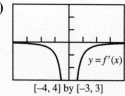

[–4, 4] by [–3, 3]

9.

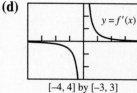

[–4, 4] by [–3, 3]

(a)

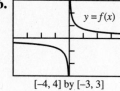

[–4, 4] by [–3, 3]

(b)

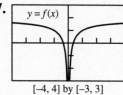

[–4, 4] by [–3, 3]

(c)

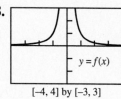

[–4, 4] by [–3, 3]

(d)

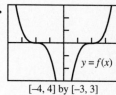

[–4, 4] by [–3, 3]

Continued

Given a graph of a function f, what would the graph of the function
$F(x) = \int_a^x f(t)\, dt$ look like? The following questions should lead you to a
rough shape of the graph of $y = F(x)$.

10. Let f be the function whose graph is shown at the right,
    and let $F(x) = \int_1^x f(t)\, dt$, for $x > 0$:

    (a) Evaluate $F(1)$. _____

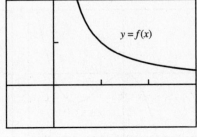

    (b) $F(x)$ is always _____
                     (increasing/decreasing)

$[-1, 3]$ by $[-1, 2]$

    (c) $F(x)$ is negative for what x values? _____

    (d) State any maximum or minimum points of $F(x)$.

    (e) Draw a rough sketch of the integral function, $F(x)$,
         on the graph at the right.

11. Let *f* be the function whose graph is shown at the right, where *f* is defined for $0 \leq x \leq 2$ and has point symmetry about $(1, 0)$

Let $F(x) = \int_0^x f(t)\, dt$.

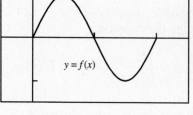

$[-0.5, 2.5]$ by $[-1.5, 1.5]$

(a) Evaluate $F(0)$. _____

(b) Evaluate $F(2)$.

(c) $F(x)$ has a maximum value at $x =$ _____

(d) $F'(x)$ has a maximum value at $x =$ _____

(e) $F'(x)$ has a minimum value at $x =$ _____

(f) $F''(x) > 0$ for what values of x? _____

(g) $F''(x) < 0$ for what values of x? _____

(h) Draw a rough sketch of the integral function, $F(x)$, on the graph to the right.

Concept Connectors

The graph of an odd function *f* is shown. Let $F(x) = \int_0^x f(t)\, dt$ and assume that $F(a) = b$.

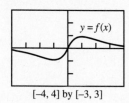

$[-4, 4]$ by $[-3, 3]$

12. Evaluate each definite integral.

(a) $\int_{-a}^{a} f(t)\, dt$ _____

(b) $\int_{-a}^{a} |f(t)|\, dt$ _____

(c) $\int_{-a}^{a} f(|t|)\, dt$ _____

13. Draw a rough sketch of the integral function $F(x) = \int_0^x f(t)\, dt$ on the same set of axes as the graph of $y = f(x)$.

5.4 Concepts Worksheet

The Fundamental Theorem of Calculus

Test your understanding of Parts 1 and 2 of the Fundamental Theorem by simplifying the following:

1. If $F(x) = \displaystyle\int_1^x \frac{dt}{1 + t^2}\, dt$, then $F'(x) =$ _____

2. If $F(x) = \displaystyle\int_3^{2x} \sqrt{t^2 + 1}\, dt$, then $F'(x) =$ _____

3. If $F(x) = \displaystyle\int_x^{2x} \frac{1}{t}\, dt,\ x > 0$, then $F'(x) =$ _____

4. If $F(x) = \displaystyle\int_0^{\sqrt{x}} \sin\left(t^2\right) dt$, then $F'(x) =$ _____

5. If $x > 0$, then $\dfrac{d}{dx} \displaystyle\int_1^{1/x} \frac{2}{t}\, dt =$ _____

6. $\displaystyle\int_1^4 \left(\frac{d}{dx} \sqrt{x^2 - 1}\right) dx =$ _____

Concept Connectors

Using the definition of a derivative and the Fundamental Theorem of Calculus, evaluate the following:

7. $\displaystyle\lim_{h \to 0} \frac{\displaystyle\int_2^{2+h} \sqrt{x^2 + x}\, dx}{h} =$ _____

_____

8. $\displaystyle\lim_{x \to 1} \frac{\displaystyle\int_1^x \frac{1}{t^4 + 1}\, dt}{x - 1} =$ _____

_____

5.5 Concepts Worksheet

Definite Integral Approximations

1. Determine and evaluate a definite integral for which
$$\frac{1}{40}[(0)^3 + 2 \cdot (0.05)^3 + 2(0.1)^3 + \cdots + 2(1.95)^3 + (2)^3]$$ is a
trapezoidal approximation. Which is greater, the integral or
trapezoidal approximation? Why?

_____

_____

2. Determine and evaluate a definite integral for which
$$\frac{1}{2}\left[\frac{1}{2} + 1.5 + 2 + 2.5 + 3 + \cdots + 9.5 + 5\right]$$ is a trapezoidal
approximation. Which is greater, the integral or the trapezoidal
approximation? Why? _____

_____

3. **(a)** Determine and evaluate a definite integral for which
$$\frac{1}{6}\left[0 + 4\left(\frac{\sqrt{2}}{2}\right) + 2(1) + 4\left(\frac{\sqrt{6}}{2}\right) + 2\sqrt{2} + 4\left(\frac{\sqrt{10}}{2}\right) + 2\sqrt{3} + 4\left(\frac{\sqrt{14}}{2}\right) + 2\right]$$
is a Simpson's Rule approximation. _____

(b) Set up the trapezoidal approximation for the integral answer
from (a) using the same number of partitions.

_____

_____

(c) Compare the Simpson's Rule and trapezoidal approximations
geometrically. Which do you think should be larger? Why?

_____

_____

Concept Connectors

4. For a strictly increasing positive-valued function over an interval
   $[a, b]$ explain why the average of the inscribed and circumscribed
   sums of the areas of n rectangles, all of constant width, is the
   trapezoidal approximation. (Note: For a strictly decreasing function
   over an interval, a similar conclusion can be obtained.)

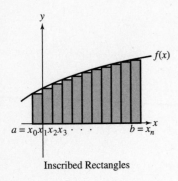

Inscribed Rectangles

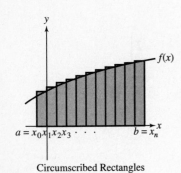

Circumscribed Rectangles

     © Addison Wesley Longman, Inc.

The Logarithmic Function

The natural logarithm can be defined as an integral function, that is:

$$\ln x = \int_1^x \frac{1}{t}\, dt,\ x > 0$$

1.

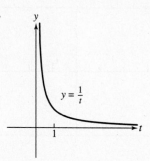

2.

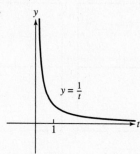

On the graph above, shade a region representing ln 2 using the definition of the definite integral.

Note: ln 2 > 0

On the graph above, shade a region representing $\ln \frac{1}{2}$ using the definition of the definite integral.

Note: $\ln \frac{1}{2} < 0$

3. Find the integral representation for the area of each shaded region below:

(a)

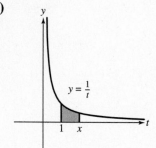

(b)

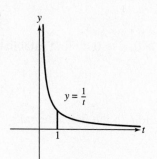

(c)

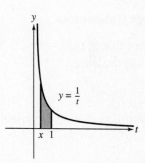

If $x > 1$, area = _____.

If $x = 1$, area = _____.

If $0 < x < 1$, area = _____.

4. Graph (Mark units on the axes.):

(a) $y = \ln(-x)$

(b) $y = \ln(1 + x)$

(c) $y = \ln(1 - x)$

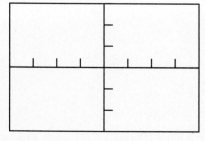

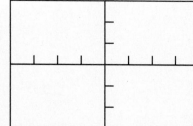

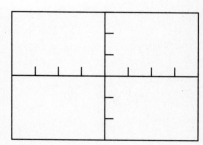

Continued

5. All of the following integrals are geometric transformations of the
ln x function. Sketch the region represented by the given integrals on
the coordinate axes below.

(a) If $x < 0$, $\int_{-1}^{x} \frac{1}{t}\,dt$ (b) If $x > -1$, $\int_{0}^{x} \frac{1}{1+t}\,dt$ (c) If $x < 1$, $\int_{0}^{x} \frac{1}{1-t}\,dt$

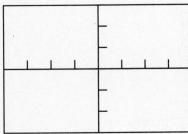 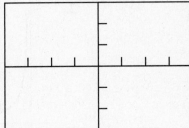 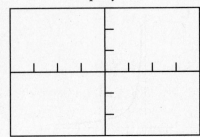

6. State an answer in terms of the natural logarithm for each of the
above:

(a) If $x < 0$, $\int_{-1}^{x} \frac{1}{t}\,dt =$ (b) If $x > -1$, $\int_{0}^{x} \frac{1}{1+t}\,dt =$ (c) If $x < 1$, $\int_{0}^{x} \frac{1}{1-t}\,dt =$

_____   _____   _____

Concept Connectors

7. Prove that ln (ax) = ln a + ln x for $x > 0$, $a > 0$ by first establishing
the equivalence.

$$\int_{a}^{ax} \frac{1}{t}\,dt = \int_{1}^{x} \frac{1}{u}\,du.$$

(Hint: Use change of variable substitution on the first integral.)

DATE

7.1–7.5 Concepts Worksheet

NAME

Integration of Rates

One of the basic concepts of integral calculus is that the integral of the rate of change of a quantity can be used to find the net change in that quantity over a period of time. For example, if $f(t)$ is the production rate of an item (in units per month, where t is in months), then $\int_4^{12} f(t)\, dt$ is equal to the number of units produced between $t = 4$ months and $t = 12$ months.

1. Let $R(t)$ represent the rate at which a tapestry is emerging from a weaver's loom. The values of $R(t)$ over a one-hour period are given below.

t(min)	0	5	10	15	20	25	30	35	40	45	50	55	60
$R(t)$(cm/min)	10	12	17	20	17	16	15	9	8	12	15	16	13

   (a) Write an integral in terms of $R(t)$ that gives the length of tapestry created during this hour.

   (b) Use a Trapezoidal Rule approximation to estimate the length of tapestry created during this hour.

2. Let $r(t)$ represent the rate of rainfall, in inches per hour, t hours after midnight, and let $f(t)$ represent the number of inches of rain that fell during the first t hours after midnight. Use the graph of $y = f(t)$ to estimate each of the following. Interpret your results by giving the real-world meaning of each integral.

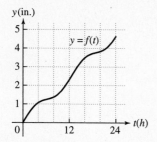

   (a) $\int_0^{24} r(t)\, dt =$ _____

   _____

   (b) $\int_4^{12} r(t)\, dt =$ _____

   _____

   (c) $\int_8^{20} r(t)\, dt =$ _____

   _____

Continued

3. From the beginning of 1985 to the beginning of 1995, a certain company earned revenues at the rate of
$r(t) = t^3 - 15t^2 + 70t + 150$ thousand dollars per year, where t is the number of years after the beginning of 1985. Find the total revenues for this ten-year period.

_____

Concept Connector

Many rates involve quantities other than time. For example, one might regard force as a rate of work done per unit of distance. In this context, the work formula $W = \int_a^b F(x)\, dx$ can be regarded as another example of a rate being integrated to find the net change of a quantity.

4. A tub weighing 20 pounds is lifted from the ground to a height of 40 feet. As the tub is being lifted, it is also being filled with pebbles so that the weight, in pounds, of the bucket when it is at height x feet is given by $20 + 3x$. Find the amount of work done in lifting the bucket and the pebbles.

7.2 Concepts Worksheet

Area as a Definite Integral

To find the area of a region R between curves, one can compute the sum of nonoverlapping rectangular areas that almost fill region R. The integral symbol, $\int$, followed by $f(x)\, dx$, evokes the notion of an infinite sum of rectangular areas having dimensions $f(x)$ and dx. For example, the region R shown on the left can be approximately filled with rectangles of height $[f(x) - g(x)]$ and width dx, as shown on the right.

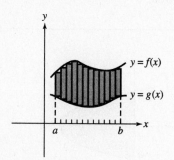
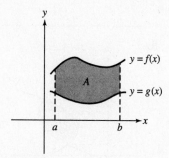

Therefore, the area of region R is: $\displaystyle\int_a^b [f(x) - g(x)]\, dx$.

Express the areas of the regions shown using definite integrals without absolute values. Where applicable, use the rectangular section shown as a guide to help you set up the correct integral expression.

1.

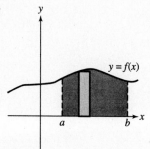

Area:

_____

2.

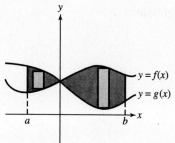

Area:

_____

3.

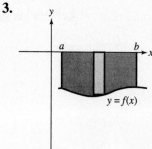

Area:

_____

Continued

4.

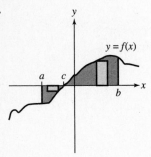

Area:

_____

5.

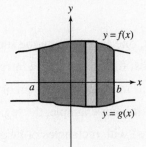

Area:

_____

6.

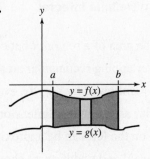

Area:

_____

7.

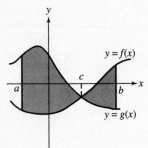

Area:

_____

8.

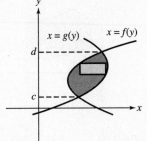

Area:

_____

9.

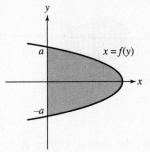

Area:

_____

Concept Connectors

10. The graph of $y^2 = 4x^2 - x^4$ is shown below.

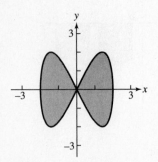

Find the area of the shaded region. _____

7.3 Concepts Worksheet

Volume as a Definite Integral

To find the volume of a solid, one can imagine that the solid is made of a stack of thin prisms or cylinders. The volume of each prism or cylinder is equal to the product of the area of a base and the height between the bases. The integral symbol, $\int$, followed by the product of face area and height, where height is an increment dx or dy, represents the volume of the solid.

Note the following examples:

A. Find the volume of the solid generated by revolving the region bounded by the graph of $y = f(x)$, the x-axis, and lines $x = a$ and $x = b$ about the x-axis.

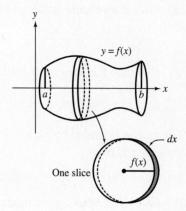

Each slice has the shape of a circle whose radius is $f(x)$. The area of this circle is $\pi[f(x)]^2$, so the volume of each cylinder is $\pi[f(x)]^2 \, dx$. The volume of the solid is $\pi \int_a^b [f(x)]^2 \, dx$.

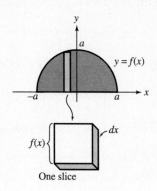

B. Suppose that the base of a solid is the shaded region shown to the right and that all cross-sections perpendicular to the x-axis are squares. Find the volume of the solid.

Each slice has the shape of a square of length $f(x)$, so the cross sectional area is $[f(x)]^2$ and the volume of each slice is $[f(x)]^2 \, dx$. The volume of the solid is $\int_{-a}^{a} [f(x)]^2 \, dx$ or, by symmetry, $2 \int_0^a [f(x)]^2 \, dx$.

Continued

1. The region bounded by $f(x) = x^2$, the x-axis, and $x = 2$ is rotated about the x-axis.

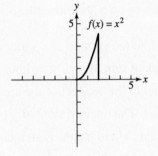

  (a) Draw the solid of revolution on the graph to the right.

  (b) Draw and label a slice made perpendicular to the x-axis.

  (c) Find the area of a cross section of the solid.

  _____

  (d) Find the volume of one slice.

  _____

  (e) Give the volume of the solid as a definite integral.

  _____

  (f) Evaluate the integral to find the volume of the solid.

  _____

2. The region bounded by $f(x) = x^2$, the x-axis, and $x = 2$ is rotated about the y-axis.

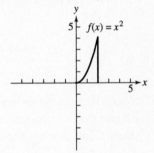

  (a) Draw the solid of revolution on the graph to the right.

  (b) Draw and label a slice made perpendicular to the y-axis.

  (c) Find the area of a cross section of the solid.

  _____

  (d) Find the volume of one slice.

  _____

  (e) Give the volume of the solid as a definite integral.

  _____

  (f) Evaluate the integral to find the volume of the solid.

  _____

Continued

3. The base of a solid is bounded by $x + 2y = 4$ and the coordinate axes. Every cross sectional slice made perpendicular to the y-axis is an isosceles right triangle with the hypotenuse on the base.

(a) Draw and label the base of the solid.

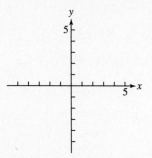

(b) Draw and label a slice made perpendicular to the y-axis.

(c) Find the area of a cross section of the solid. _____

(d) Find the volume of one slice. _____

(e) Give the volume of the solid as a definite integral. _____

(f) Find the volume of the solid. _____

Concept Connectors

The method of computing volume by cylindrical shells may seem very different from the approach above, but the concepts being applied are related. In Figure 1 the plane region bounded by $y = f(x)$ and the lines $x = a$ and $x = b$ is rotated about the y-axis. Imagine the rectangle drawn in Figure 1 being rotated about the y-axis. It generates a cylindrical shell as shown in Figure 2.

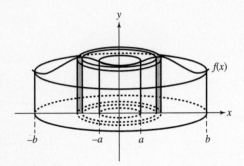

Figure 1

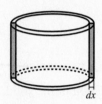

Figure 2

If we slice the wall of the cylindrical shell perpendicular to its bases, unfold and lay it flat, then we obtain a rectangular solid as in Figure 3.

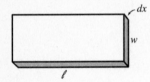

Figure 3

4. (a) Express w in terms of x and/or $f(x)$.

_____

(b) Express l in terms of x and/or $f(x)$.

_____

(c) Find the face area, lw. _____

(d) Give the volume of the solid drawn in Figure 3.

_____

(e) Give the volume of the solid drawn in Figure 1 as a definite integral.

_____

Power Series and Taylor's Theorem

1. (a) If $f(x) = \displaystyle\sum_{n=1}^{\infty} \frac{(-1)^{n+1}(2x)^n}{n}$ for what values of x does the series converge? _____

(b) Write the first three terms and the nth term of the series representing $f\left(\dfrac{1}{4}\right)$ in part (a) above.

_____

(c) Evaluate $f\left(\dfrac{1}{4}\right)$ by relating it to an appropriate Maclaurin Series.

_____

(d) Write a series expansion for $f'(x)$ and evaluate $f'\left(\dfrac{1}{4}\right)$.

_____

2. Let f be a function that has derivatives of all orders on the open interval $(2.5, 3.5)$. Assume that $f(3) = 7, f'(3) = -3, f''(3) = 12$ and $|f'''(x)| \le 36$ for all x in the interval $(2.5, 3.5)$.

(a) Find the second-order Taylor polynomial about $x = 3$ for $f(x)$.

_____

(b) Use your answer to part (a) to estimate the value of $f(2.7)$.

_____

What is the maximum possible error in making this estimate?

_____

(c) Let $h(x)$ be a function that has the properties $h(3) = -2$ and $h'(x) = f(x)$. Find the Maclaurin series for $h(x)$.
(Write as many nonzero terms as possible.)

_____

(d) Let $g(x) = x^2 f(x + 3)$. Find the Maclaurin series for $g(x)$.
(Write as many nonzero terms as possible.)

_____

Concept Connector

3. Let $f(x) = 3 + 5x - \dfrac{3}{2!}x^2 - \dfrac{5}{3!}x^3 + \dfrac{3}{4!}x^4 + \dfrac{5}{5!}x^5 - \dfrac{3}{6!}x^6 - \dfrac{5}{7!}x^7 + \cdots$

$$+ (-1)^n\left[\dfrac{3}{(2n)!}x^{2n} + \dfrac{5}{(2n+1)!}x^{2n+1}\right] + \cdots$$

(a) Show that $y = f(x)$ is a solution to the differential equation $y'' + y = 0$.

_____

_____

_____

_____

(b) Find the domain of the function f. _____

(c) Write a closed-form expression for $f(x)$ in terms of basic functions. (Hint: Look at the odd-numbered terms and the even-numbered terms separately.)

_____

10.3 Concepts Worksheet

Vector Functions and Motion

As an overview of concepts related to vector functions and motion, consider the following questions:

1. (a) A vector is tangent to the curve $y = x^2$ at the vector's initial point. If the vector contains the point $(0, -2)$, find all possibilities for the vector's initial point.

(b) A vector is normal to the curve $y = x^2$ at the vector's initial point. If the vector contains the point $(0, -2)$, find all possibilities for the vector's initial point.

(c) A vector is normal to the curve $y = x^2$ at the vector's initial point. If the vector contains the point $(0, 2)$, find all possibilities for the vector's initial point.

(d) Graphically illustrate parts (a), (b), and (c) on the graph below. Use this graph to help you decide whether you have found all the points requested in each part.

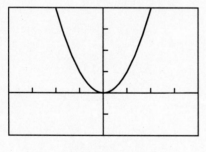

[–4, 4] by [–2, 4]

2. $\mathbf{r}(t) = (2 - \sin t)\mathbf{i} + (3 \cos t)\mathbf{j}$ gives the position of a particle at any time t, $0 \le t \le 2\pi$.

(a) Find the particle's velocity and acceleration vectors at time $t = \dfrac{\pi}{6}$.

Continued

(b) Sketch the path given by **r**(t) and vectors representing $\mathbf{r}'\left(\dfrac{\pi}{6}\right)$ and $\mathbf{r}''\left(\dfrac{\pi}{6}\right)$.

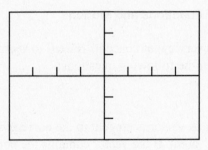

(c) Find the times, t, at which the speed of the particle is:

a minimum: $t = $ _____

a maximum: $t = $ _____

3. If $\mathbf{r}'(t) = 2t\mathbf{i} + 3t^2\mathbf{j}$ and $\mathbf{r}(1) = \mathbf{i}$

(a) $\mathbf{r}(t) = $ _____

(b) Sketch the path given by **r**(t).

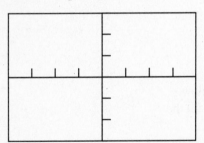

(c) Evaluate and sketch $\mathbf{r}'(1)$ on the graph in (b).

_____

(d) Find and sketch in (b) any horizontal $\mathbf{r}''(t)$ vectors.

_____

(e) Find and sketch in (b) any vertical $\mathbf{r}''(t)$ vectors.

_____

Concept Connectors

4. (a) Cite an example of particle motion $\mathbf{r}(t)$, where $\mathbf{r}(t) = \mathbf{r}'(t)$.

_____

(b) Cite an example of particle motion, $\mathbf{r}(t)$, where $\mathbf{r}(t) = -\mathbf{r}'(t)$.

_____

10.5 Concepts Worksheet

Families of Polar Curves

There are famous families of curves in the polar-coordinate system with polar equations that are easily recognizable. Review the following generalizations and complete the graphs as indicated.

1. Family of Lines

The rectangular form of a line $ax + by = c$ translates in polar form to $ar \cos \theta + br \sin \theta = c$. The following are often-used special cases of linear equations. Sketch each line if $c = 1$.

(a) $r \cos \theta = c$ or $r = c \sec \theta$ **(b)** $r \sin \theta = c$ or $r = c \csc \theta$ **(c)** $\theta = c$

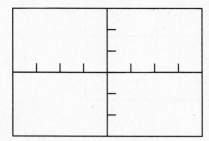 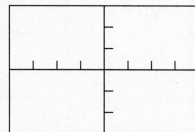 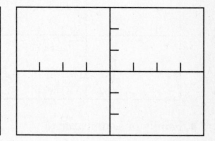

2. Family of Circles

The rectangular form of a line $x^2 + y^2 = a^2$, with center at the origin, translates in polar form to $r = a$. If the center is not at the pole, then the following forms are common. Sketch each circle if $a = 2$ and $b = 1$.

(a) $r = a \cos \theta$ **(b)** $r = a \sin \theta$ **(c)** $r = a \cos \theta + b \sin \theta$

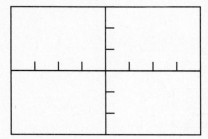 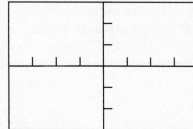 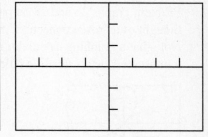

3. Family of Roses

A rose has no easily recognizable rectangular form but in polar form can be generally described as $r = a \cos(n\theta)$ or $r = a \sin(n\theta)$, where n is a natural number. If n is even, the rose has $2n$ petals and $4n$ lines of symmetry; if n is odd, the rose has n petals and n lines of symmetry.

Sketch:

(a) $r = 2 \cos 3\theta$

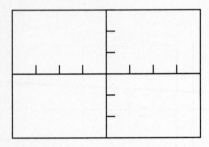

(b) $r = -3 \sin 2\theta$

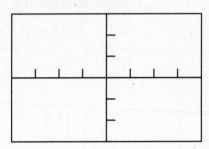

4. Family of Lemniscates

Polar form: $r^2 = a^2 \cos 2\theta$
$r^2 = a^2 \sin 2\theta$

Note similarities to the four-petaled rose: $r = a \cos 2\theta$ or $r = a \sin 2\theta$.

For example, $r = a \cos 2\theta$ would "lose" two petals on becoming $r^2 = a^2 \cos 2\theta$, namely, the petals with axis of symmetry $\theta = \dfrac{\pi}{2}$.

Actually, the shape of a lemniscate's petals is different (compare Problem graphs 25 and 28 on page 558 of the textbook), but the thought of a "rose connection" may assist in sketching graphs. Note that a graphing calculator is likely to "cut off" the portions of a lemniscate's petals near the pole, depending on the θ-interval chosen.

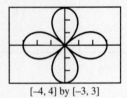

[−4, 4] by [−3, 3]

$r = 3 \cos 2\theta$

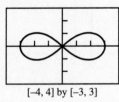

[−4, 4] by [−3, 3]

$r^2 = 9 \cos 2\theta$

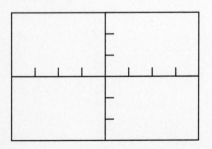

Sketch: $r^2 = 4 \sin 2\theta$

Continued

5. Family of Limaçons

Polar form: $r = a \pm b \cos \theta$ or
                    $r = a \pm b \sin \theta$

The shapes of limaçons depend on the values of a and b used in the equations above.

If $|a| = |b|$, then the limaçon includes the pole, and either $r \geq 0$ for the entire curve, or $r \leq 0$ for the entire curve.

Examples:

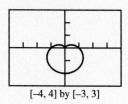
[−4, 4] by [−3, 3]

$r = 1 - \sin \theta$
Note: $r \geq 0$

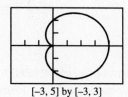
[−3, 5] by [−3, 3]

$r = -2 + 2 \cos \theta$
Note: $r \leq 0$

If $|a| > |b|$, then either $r > 0$ for the entire curve, or $r < 0$ for the entire curve. These limaçons do not include the pole.

Examples:

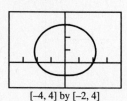
[−4, 4] by [−2, 4]

$r = 2 + \sin \theta$
Note: $r > 0$

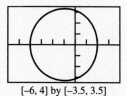
[−6, 4] by [−3.5, 3.5]

$r = -3 - \cos \theta$
Note: $r < 0$

If $|a| < |b|$, then the limaçon involves both positive and negative values of r and the limaçon has an "inner loop".

Example:

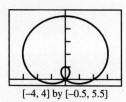
[−4, 4] by [−0.5, 5.5]

$r = 2 + 3 \sin \theta$

Continued

Sketch:

(a) $r = \cos\theta - 1$ **(b)** $r = 1 + 2\sin\theta$ **(c)** $r = 2 - \cos\theta$

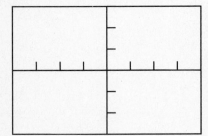 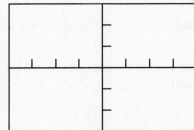 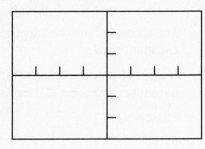

Concept Connector

6. The concept of equations in polar form is closely related to the concept of parametric equations. Any equation in the form $r = f(\theta)$ has the same graph as the parametric equations $x = f(\theta)\cos\theta$, $y = f(\theta)\sin\theta$.

For each parametrization below, sketch the graph of the parametrized curve and give the equation in polar form.

(a) 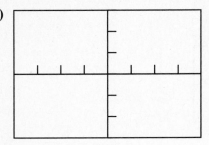   **(b)**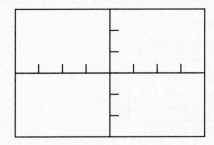

$x = (2 + \sin t)\cos t$ $x = 2\cos t \sin 5t$
$y = (2 + \sin t)\sin t$ $y = 2\sin t \sin 5t$
$0 \le t \le 2\pi$ $0 \le t \le 2\pi$

Polar form: _____   Polar form: _____

10.6 Concepts Worksheet

Tangent and Normal Lines to Polar Curves

To write an equation of a tangent line to a curve, one must know the coordinates of the point of tangency and the slope of the tangent at that point.

Since the slope of a curve has been defined as $\dfrac{dy}{dx}$, the slope of a polar curve can be found by converting the equation to parametric form. That is, if the polar curve is described as $r = f(\theta)$, then a corresponding parametric form is $x = f(\theta) \cos \theta$ and $y = f(\theta) \sin \theta$.

The slope of the tangent is $\dfrac{dy}{dx}$, where $\dfrac{dy}{dx} = \dfrac{dy/d\theta}{dx/d\theta}$.

Complete the following problems.

1. $r = 1 + \cos \theta$

   (a) Parametric equations $x = $ _____

                                     $y = $ _____

   (b) $\dfrac{dx}{d\theta} = $ _____

         $\dfrac{dy}{d\theta} = $ _____

   (c) Tangent slope, $\dfrac{dy}{dx} = $ _____

   (d) Cartesian equation of tangent line at $\theta = \dfrac{\pi}{2}$: _____

   (e) Cartesian equation of normal line at $\theta = \dfrac{\pi}{2}$: _____

2. $r = -\cos \theta$

   (a) Parametric equations $x = $ _____

                                       $y = $ _____

   (b) $\dfrac{dx}{d\theta} = $ _____

         $\dfrac{dy}{d\theta} = $ _____

   (c) Tangent slope, $\dfrac{dy}{dx} = $ _____

   (d) Find the values of θ, $0 \le \theta \le \pi$, at which tangent lines are horizontal.

     _____

   (e) Find the values of θ, $0 \le \theta \le \pi$, at which tangent lines are vertical.

     _____

Continued

3. Orthogonal curves have perpendicular tangent lines at any points of intersection. Prove that $r = 2 \cos \theta$ and $r = 2 \sin \theta$ are orthogonal curves at their points of intersection.

Concept Connectors

4. Graphs of limaçons of the type $r = a \pm b \cos \theta$ or $r = a \pm b \sin \theta$, where $|a| > |b|$, have a subtle, graphical interest at the point on the curve which is nearest the pole. The relationship of a to b determines whether the graph undergoes a change in concavity in a neighborhood of the point nearest the pole. It appears to "dimple" for certain values of a and b. For example, consider the graph of $r = \dfrac{6}{5} - \sin \theta$.

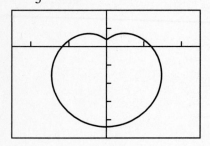

[–2.5, 2.5] by [–2.5, 1]

One of the ways to convince ourselves of this phenomenon would be to search for all of the horizontal tangent lines of $r = \dfrac{6}{5} - \sin \theta$.

(a) Find values of θ, $0 \le \theta \le 2\pi$, such that $\dfrac{dy}{dx} = 0$.

(b) Sketch the horizontal tangents on the graph above. You should locate four tangent lines at roughly the same θ values obtained in part (a).

5. Sketch a graph of $r = 2 + \cos \theta$. Does this graph have "dimple" at the point closest to the pole? Explain.

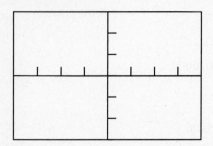

6. For the special case $r = a + \sin \theta$, determine for what values of $a \ge 1$ the graph appears to "dimple".

Letterboxes: You Could Be a Winner!

The purpose of this Exploration is to review some of the important functions found in Chapter 1, while perhaps providing some surprises along the way. The object of the game is to fill in all the squares. (If you feel up to a little extra challenge, try doing it without a calculator.)

A	B	C	D	E	F
G	H	I	J	K	L
M	N	O	P	Q	R
S	T	U	V	W	X

1. Pick a whole number between (but not including) 2 and 9. Write it in Box A.

2. Multiply the number in Box A by 9 and write the second digit of the result in Box B.

3. Add the number in Box A to the number in Box B and write the sum in Box C.

4. Write your age in Box D.

5. Take the common logarithm of the number in Box C and write it in Box E.

6. Using the number in Box A as slope and the number in Box E as y-intercept, write an equation of a line in Box F.

7. Find the x-intercept of the line in Box F and write it in Box G.

8. Using the number in Box G as slope and the number in Box D as y-intercept, write the equation of a line in Box H.

9. Evaluate the function in Box H at the number in Box A. Subtract the result from the number in Box D and write the difference in Box I.

10. Find the absolute value of the number in Box G and write it in Box J.

Review Group Activity Exploration NAME

11. Divide the natural logarithm of the number in Box J by the natural logarithm of the number in Box A, and write the result in Box K.

12. Find the letter of the box that contains the largest number in the grid so far. Think of a European country beginning with that letter and write it in Box L.

13. Take the second letter of the country in Box L. Think of a one-digit number beginning with that letter and write that number in Box M.

14. Find the sine and the cosine of the number in Box M. Square these two numbers and write the sum of the squares in Box N.

15. Write the number in Box C as a word. Change a single letter of the word to get the name of a trig function. Write that function in Box O.

16. Find the period of the function in Box O and write it in Box P.

17. Multiply the number in Box A by the number in Box P. Plug the product into the function in Box O and write the function value in Box Q.

18. Find the product of all the numbers in the grid so far and write that product in Box R.

19. Raise the number in Box A to the power of the number in Box R. Write the result in Box S.

20. Add the number in Box M to the number in Box S and multiply the sum by the number in Box D. Write this product in Box T.

Review **Group Activity Exploration** NAME

21. Add the digits of the number in Box T together. If the result is a single digit, write it in Box U. If the result is two digits, add those two digits together and write the sum in Box U.

22. There is one number that appears in every row of the grid. The letters that correspond to the boxes containing that number can be rearranged to spell a function. Write that function in Box V.

23. Find the number in the grid that rhymes with the function in Box V. Write the letter of the Box containing that number in Box W.

24. Find the angle of intersection (in radians) of the two lines in Boxes F and H. Evaluate the function in Box V at that angle and write the function value in Box X.

    If you have successfully filled in all the letterboxes, read the contents of the last two aloud and hear our special message to you!

2.3 Group Activity Exploration

Salt-and-Pepper Functions

The functions that we deal with in calculus are usually continuous throughout their domains, but we gain a better understanding of continuity (and of limits in general) by understanding how functions *fail* to be continuous. A function that is particularly impressive in that respect is the characteristic function on the rational numbers, defined as follows:

$$f(x) = \begin{cases} 1, & \text{if } x \text{ is rational} \\ 0, & \text{if } x \text{ is irrational} \end{cases}.$$

This function is discontinuous at *every* real number (Exercise 49, Section 2.3). It is sometimes referred to informally as a *salt-and-pepper function* because its graph consists of disjoint "salt" points corresponding to rational x-values (along the line $y = 1$) and "pepper" points corresponding to irrational x-values (along the line $y = 0$). It is impossible to produce a true graph of this function, but we can imagine it being something like this:

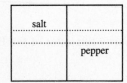

The "holes" in the line $y = 1$ occur at irrational x-values and lie directly above points of the graph that lie on the x-axis.

In this exploration you will use the "salt-and-pepper" technique to construct some functions with properties you might never have thought to be possible.

A. Consider the salt-and-pepper function

$$f(x) = \begin{cases} x, & \text{if } x \text{ is rational} \\ 0, & \text{if } x \text{ is irrational} \end{cases}$$

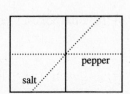

1. Explain why $\lim_{x \to 0} f(x) = 0$ if x takes on only irrational values. (Follow the pepper points.)

2. Explain why $\lim_{x \to 0} f(x) = 0$ if x takes on only rational values. (Follow the salt points.)

3. Let *a* be any real number other than zero. Explain why $\lim_{x \to a} f(x) = 0$ if *x* takes on only irrational values, but $\lim_{x \to a} f(x) = a$ if *x* takes on only rational values.

4. Explain why we can conclude that *f* is a function with domain all real numbers that is *continuous only at* $x = 0$.

B. Consider the salt-and-pepper function

$$f(x) = \begin{cases} \sin x, & \text{if } x \text{ is rational} \\ 0, & \text{if } x \text{ is irrational} \end{cases}.$$

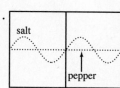

1. Explain why *f* is only continuous at integer multiples of π.

2. By adjusting the period of the "salt" curve, construct a function with domain all reals that is *continuous at every integer* and *discontinuous* everywhere else.

3. We have already seen a function with domain all reals that is *discontinuous at every integer* and *continuous* everywhere else. Can you think of what it is?

Continued

C. Construct salt-and-pepper functions that have domain all reals and are continuous *only* on the following sets:

1. $\{-2, 2\}$

2. $\{-1, 0, 1\}$

3. the even integers

D. Discuss the continuity of the salt-and-pepper function

$$f(x) = \begin{cases} 0, & \text{if } x \text{ is rational} \\ \sin(\pi/x), & \text{if } x \text{ is irrational} \end{cases}.$$

3.1 Group Activity Exploration

Identifying a Function by its Properties

Suppose you know that a continuous function f with domain all real numbers satisfies the following two properties:

(a) $f(x + h) = f(x) + f(h) + 2xh$ for all real numbers x and h;

(b) $\lim\limits_{h \to 0} \dfrac{f(h)}{h} = 10$.

Can you identify the function?

1. Use the definition of the derivative and the two given properties to show that $f'(x) = 10 + 2x$.

2. Construct a polynomial that has derivative $10 + 2x$.

3. There are infinitely many polynomials that have derivative $10 + 2x$. Construct one that is different from your answer above.

4. How would you describe *all* functions that have derivative $10 + 2x$?

5. Show that property (a) implies that $f(0) = 0$.

6. Combine the results from #4 and #5 to identify the unique function f that satisfies all of the given properties.

7. As a check on your answer, show that your function f satisfies property (a).

8. Change the "$2xh$" in property (a) to "$4xh$." What effect does this have on the solution in **6**?

9. Change the "10" in property (b) to "20." What effect does this have on the solution in **6**?

10. Identify the continuous function f with domain all real numbers that satisfies the following two properties (where A and B are nonzero constants):

(a) $f(x + h) = f(x) + f(h) + Axh$ for all real numbers x and h;

(b) $\lim\limits_{h \to 0} \dfrac{f(h)}{h} = B$.

4.4 Group Activity Exploration

Thinking about Optimization

The fuel consumption rate C (in gallons per hour) of a certain automobile as a function of its velocity v (in miles per hour) is modeled by the equation

$$C(v) = v^4 \times 10^{-7} - 0.02v + 1.5.$$

The model is effective for velocities in the domain $0 < v < 70$.

1. Graph this function in the window $[-7.5, 70]$ by $[-0.25, 2]$ and copy it carefully into the window provided below. Label the units on both axes.

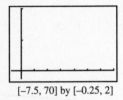

[−7.5, 70] by [−0.25, 2]

2. Notice that the function decreases at first, then increases. From what you know about automobiles, does this behavior make sense?

3. Find the critical point on the graph. What quantity is optimized at this point?

4. For efficient driving, we should seek to minimize the number of *gallons per mile*. (This is equivalent to maximizing the reciprocal, which is miles per gallon.) Choose a point (x, y) on your graph of C as a function of v. Explain why y/x gives the number of *gallons per mile* consumed by the car at that point.

5. Draw a line through your chosen point (x, y) and the origin. What quantity does the slope of this line represent?

6. Is the fuel consumption in gallons per mile minimized at the critical point found in step 3? Geometrically, how can you tell?

Continued

7. At what point on the curve will the fuel consumption (in gallons per mile) be minimized? Identify the point on your curve geometrically.

8. Use calculus to find this point algebraically, thereby showing that the velocity that optimizes fuel efficiency in this particular model is approximately 47 MPH.

9. It has been argued that calculus is no longer needed to solve optimization problems now that calculators will find minimum points on curves. What does this exploration suggest about that argument?

10. The energy used by a swimming shark (in calories per hour) as a function of its swimming speed (in miles per hour) has a graph with the same shape as the function $C(v)$ discussed above. Explain why this is so.

11. Does the graph help explain why you never see sharks staying still in the water?

12. Does it benefit a shark more to minimize its energy consumption in terms of calories per *hour* or calories per *mile*, or would it depend on the circumstances? In which case would the shark need to be swimming faster?

5.4 Group Activity Exploration

The Volume of a Right Circular Cone

The 3-dimensional figure we usually think of as a "cone" is more carefully referred to as a "right circular cone" because its altitude is perpendicular to its base, which is circular. You probably learned in a geometry class that the formula for the volume of such a cone is

$$V = \frac{1}{3}\pi r^2 h,$$

where r and h are the radius of the base and the height, respectively. In this exploration you will derive this formula as a limit of Riemann sums evaluated as a definite integral; then you will extend the formula to a more general cone. (An exploration in Chapter 7 generalizes this formula still further.)

1. Orient the cone on the coordinate axes so that its vertex is at the origin and its altitude lies along the x-axis, as shown at the right. If the cone has radius r and height h, what are the coordinates of point P?

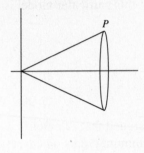

2. Let x_k be any number between 0 and h. The cross-sectional slice of the cone that intersects the x-axis at x_k is circular. Use similar triangles to show that the radius of this circular slice is $\frac{r}{h}x_k$.

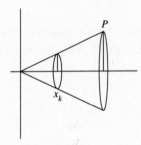

3. If we give this circular slice a bit of thickness Δx, then it becomes a thin cylindrical disk. Use the formula for the volume of a cylinder to show that the volume of the disk is $\pi\left(\frac{r}{h}x_k\right)^2 \Delta x$.

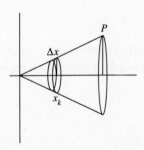

Continued

4. Approximate the volume of the entire cone as a Riemann sum of the volumes of these cylindrical disks, and show that the limit of such Riemann sums is the definite integral

$$\int_0^h \frac{\pi r^2}{h^2} x^2 \, dx.$$

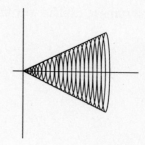

5. Explain why $\int_0^h \frac{\pi r^2}{h^2} x^2 \, dx = \frac{\pi r^2}{h^2} \int_0^h x^2 \, dx$. Is it always safe to move a part of the integrand outside the integral?

6. Use the Fundamental Theorem to evaluate the integral.

7. Suppose that all the disks in the figure shown in step 4 were shifted vertically downward so that they were tangent to the x-axis at their highest point. The same Riemann sum would then become an approximation to the volume of a different solid, an *oblique* circular cone. What are the radius and height of this oblique circular cone?

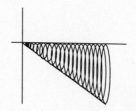

Continued

8. Use Riemann sums to explain why the volume of the oblique circular cone thus formed should also be

$$\int_0^h \frac{\pi r^2}{h^2} x^2 \, dx.$$

9. What is the formula for the volume of an oblique circular cone? Identify in a drawing of the solid all variables that appear in your formula.

6.1 Group Activity Exploration

Reading Slope Fields

A slope field gives us useful information about the solution to a differential equation even when we are unable to "solve" the differential equation itself. You might someday take a course that is devoted almost exclusively to finding explicit solutions to differential equations, but for now most such solutions are beyond your reach.

Nonetheless, try this exploration to see how well you can match a differential equation to its slope field purely on the basis of the differential equation itself. (If you have a program in your calculator that produces slope fields, this is not the time to use it. Also, do not attempt to *solve* the differential equations; they are much harder to solve than they look.)

I. One of the following slope fields is for the differential equation $\frac{dy}{dx} = x + y$, and the other is for the differential equation $\frac{dy}{dx} = x - y$.

A 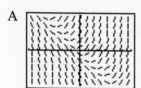   B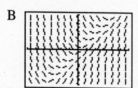

1. Where would you expect the slope to be zero in the slope field for $\frac{dy}{dx} = x + y$? Where would you expect the slope to be zero in the slope field for $\frac{dy}{dx} = x - y$?

2. Which slope field goes with which equation?

3. Why do the slopes shown on either slope field increase as you move to the right along a horizontal line?

II. One of the following slope fields is for the differential equation $\frac{dy}{dx} = 1.1^{x^2}$, and the other is for the differential equation $\frac{dy}{dx} = 1.1^{y^2}$.

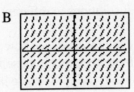

A   B

1. Why do all the slope lines represent a function with positive slope?

2. Which slope field shows slopes that depend on x but not on y? Which slope field shows slopes that depend on y but not on x?

3. Which slope field goes with which equation?

4. Would you expect solutions to these differential equations to be odd functions, even functions, or neither? Explain.

III. One of the following slope fields is for the differential equation $\frac{dy}{dx} = \sin(y^2)$, and the other is for the differential equation $\frac{dy}{dx} = \sin(y^3)$.

A 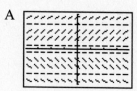   B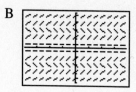

1. Why do both graphs exhibit horizontal patterns?

2. Which slope field goes with which equation? How can you tell?

3. Would you be able to distinguish between the slope fields for $\frac{dy}{dx} = \cos(y^2)$ and $\frac{dy}{dx} = \cos(y^3)$ in the same way? Explain.

IV. One of the following slope fields is for the differential equation $\dfrac{dy}{dx} = \sin{(xy)}$, and the other is for the differential equation $\dfrac{dy}{dx} = \cos{(xy)}$.

A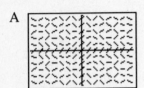

B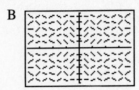

1. Which slope field goes with which equation?

2. Explain how the behavior of the slope lines along the axes helps to identify the correct equation.

3. Explain how the symmetry of the graph helps to identify the correct equation.

7.3 Group Activity Exploration

The Volume of a General Cone

In 5.4 Group Activity Exploration you derived the formula for the volume of a right circular cone:

$$V = \frac{1}{3}\pi r^2 h,$$

where r and h are the radius of the base and the height, respectively. Notice that this formula can be broken down as

$$V = \frac{1}{3} \cdot \text{(area of base)} \cdot \text{(height)}.$$

It is an interesting (and long-known) fact that this formula applies to *any* conical figure, no matter how irregular the shape of its 2-dimensional base. The "cone" can be formed by constructing a line segment from each point on the perimeter of the base to a single vertex point. If A is the area of the base and h is the distance from the vertex to the plane containing the base, then the formula for the volume of the cone is

$$V = \frac{1}{3}Ah.$$

In this exploration, you will derive this formula using the same Riemann sum strategy as was used in the 5.4 exploration.

1. Orient the cone on the coordinate axes so that its vertex is at the origin and its base is perpendicular to the x-axis at $x = h$.

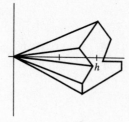

2. Let x_k be any number between 0 and h. The cross-sectional slice of the cone that intersects the x-axis at x_k is geometrically similar to the base, but smaller. Use similar triangles to show that, compared to the base of the cone, the smaller figure is shrunk vertically by a factor of $\frac{x_k}{h}$.

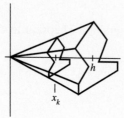

3. Explain why the smaller figure must also be shrunk *horizontally* by a factor of $\frac{x_k}{h}$.

4. Use steps 2 and 3 to show that the area of the cross section is $\left(\frac{x_k}{h}\right)^2$ times the area of the base.

5. If we give this irregular slice a thickness Δx, then it becomes
   a thin slab with volume Δx times its area. Show that the
   volume of the slab is $A\left(\dfrac{x_k}{h}\right)^2 \Delta x$, where A is the area
   of the cone's base.

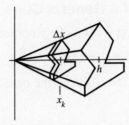

6. Approximate the volume of the entire cone as a Riemann sum of the volumes of these thin slabs, and
   show that the limit of such Riemann sums is the definite integral

   $$\int_0^h \frac{A}{h^2} x^2 \, dx.$$

7. Explain why $\displaystyle\int_0^h \frac{A}{h^2} x^2 \, dx = \frac{A}{h^2} \int_0^h x^2 \, dx$. What property of definite integrals is being used here?

8. Use the Fundamental Theorem to evaluate the integral .

9. If the base is a polygon, the cone is a special kind of polyhedron called a *pyramid*. Use the formula you
   have just derived for the volume of a general cone to find the specific formula for the volume of a pyramid
   with height h and:

   (a) a square base of side s;

   (b) an equilateral triangular base of side s;

   (c) a regular hexagonal base of side s.

8.3 Group Activity Exploration

Improper Integrals on a Calculator

Can a calculator find an improper integral such as $\int_{-\infty}^{\infty} e^{-(x^2/2)}\, dx$?

Since numerical integral programs like NINT compute definite integrals over finite intervals, most such programs would be unable to handle input like "NINT($e\wedge(-x^2/2)$, x, $-\infty$, ∞)." Still, every improper integral is the limit of definite integrals over finite intervals, so we can use NINT to evaluate those definite integrals and see if they approach a limit. (See Example 6 in the textbook.)

In this exploration we will see just how far we can go using NINT on an improper integral.

1. The graph in the window $[-4, 4]$ by $[0, 1.1]$ suggests that $y = e^{(-x^2/2)}$ is bounded above by $y = e^{-x}$ for all $x > 2$, and we know that $\int_{2}^{\infty} e^{-x}\, dx$ converges. Explain why it follows that $\int_{-\infty}^{\infty} e^{-(x^2/2)}\, dx$ converges.

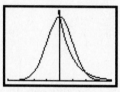

[−4, 4] by [0, 1.1]

2. Since $\int_{-\infty}^{\infty} e^{-(x^2/2)}\, dx$ converges, the definite integrals $\int_{-N}^{\infty} e^{-(x^2/2)}\, dx$ approach a limit as $N \to \infty$. Find NINT($e\wedge(-x^2/2)$, x, $-N$, N) for the following values of N: 4, 6, and 8.

3. Now find NINT($e\wedge(-x^2/2)$, x, $-N$, N) for the following values of N: 40, 60, 80.

4. What can you conclude about the limit as $N \to \infty$? Can you say that you have found the *exact* value of the improper integral?

Continued

5. The exact value of the improper integral is actually a number you might recognize. Can you recognize it based on the calculator's answer?

6. Square the calculator's answer. Do you recognize it now?

7. Divide the square by 2. Now do you recognize it? What do you conclude is the exact value of

$$\int_{-\infty}^{\infty} e^{-(x^2/2)} \, dx?$$

8. Now find NINT($e^\wedge(-x^2/2)$, x, $-N$, N) for the following values of N: 4000, 6000, 8000. Are you surprised by the calculator's answers?

     The results obtained in step 8 of this exploration show once again that numerical programs can go awry under unusual circumstances. Remember that NINT computes definite integrals by finding sums over smaller and smaller partitions of the interval of integration. The NINT program knows when to quit in the same way that you knew when to quit in step 3 of this exploration, when 40, 60, and 80 all gave the same result. When your calculator gets the same result for an approximating sum after narrowing the partition a few times, it concludes that it has reached the limit (at least within the pre-programmed tolerance). So what happened in step 8? Continue this exploration to find out.

9. Imagine using MRAM to find NINT($e^\wedge(-x^2/2)$, x, -6000, 6000). If you were to use 100 rectangles, how *wide* would each rectangle be?

10. The largest MRAM rectangles would be the ones closest to the origin. One of these would cover the interval $[-120, 0]$; the other would cover the interval $[0, 120]$. Using your calculator, plug the midpoints of these intervals into the function to find the heights of these rectangles.

11. Using the heights calculated in step 10, calculate the areas of the rectangles. Remember: These are the largest ones that MRAM will encounter. What will be the sum of all the MRAM rectangles?

12. Repeat steps 9 through 11 for 150 rectangles. Does the MRAM sum change? How about for 200 rectangles?

13. Now can you explain how the calculator might have been fooled into giving the wrong answer for NINT($e^\wedge(-x^2/2)$, x, -6000, 6000)?

9.2 Group Activity Exploration

Odds and Evens

Recall that an *odd* function is one for which $f(x)$ and $f(-x)$ are always opposites, and an *even* function is one for which $f(x)$ and $f(-x)$ are always equal. It is particularly simple to identify odd or even polynomial functions, since they are exactly the ones with (respectively) all odd powers of x or all even powers of x.

Most functions we encounter (including most polynomial functions) are neither odd nor even. However, you can *split* any polynomial into the sum of an odd function and an even function by simply separating the powers, e.g.:

$$4x^7 + 7x^6 - 12x^3 - 3x^2 + 8x - 5 = (4x^7 - 12x^3 + 8x) + (7x^6 - 3x^2 - 5)$$

Can you split *any* function this way? For example, does $f(x) = e^x$ have an odd component and an even component? Try this exploration.

1. Let $T(x)$ denote the Taylor series for e^x at $x = 0$:

$$T(x) = 1 + x + \frac{x^2}{2!} + \frac{x^3}{3!} + \cdots + \frac{x^n}{n!} + \cdots.$$

This series converges absolutely for all x.

Find two series $T_O(x)$ and $T_E(x)$ such that $T(x) = T_O(x) + T_E(x)$, and $T_O(x)$ is odd and $T_E(x)$ is even.

2. Show that $T_E(x) = \dfrac{T(x) + T(-x)}{2}$.

3. Show that $T_O(x) = \dfrac{T(x) - T(-x)}{2}$.

4. What trig function has an expansion similar to $T_E(x)$? In what respect do the two expansions differ?

Continued

5. What trig function has an expansion similar to $T_O(x)$? In what respect do the two expansions differ?

6. $T_E(x)$ converges for all x to the function $\dfrac{e^x + e^{-x}}{2}$, called the *hyperbolic cosine* of x, denoted cosh x.

   $T_O(x)$ converges to the *hyperbolic sine* of x, denoted sinh x. Find the formula for sinh x.

7. Show (without using power series) that e^x splits into even and odd components as $e^x = \cosh x + \sinh x$.

8. Show (without using power series) that *any* function f splits into even and odd components as

   $\dfrac{f(x) + f(-x)}{2} + \dfrac{f(x) - f(-x)}{2}$. (Note that either of these components could be zero if the function is already

   even or odd. Also, the domain of these components may be smaller than the domain of f.)

9. Use the formula in step 8 to show that the even and odd components of $f(x) = \dfrac{1}{1-x}$ are $\dfrac{1}{1-x^2}$ and $\dfrac{x}{1-x^2}$ respectively.

10. Find the Maclaurin series for $\dfrac{x}{1-x^2}$ and $\dfrac{1}{1-x^2}$ and verify that their sum (assuming that $|x| < 1$) is equal

    to the Maclaurin series for $\dfrac{1}{1-x}$.

11. Assuming that $|x| < 1$, show that the even powers in the Maclaurin series for ln $(x + 1)$ converge to

    ln $\sqrt{1 - x^2}$. To what function do the odd powers converge?

10.6 Group Activity Exploration

A Rose is a Rose is a Rose

Exploration 2 in Section 10.5 introduces you to the polar curves described by mathematicians as rose curves. (That exploration continues in Exercise 64 at the end of the section.) In this exploration we will look at the areas of various rose curves and prove an interesting generalization by the method of substitution.

1. In POLAR mode, set the window on your grapher to $[-3, 3]$ by $[-2, 2]$, and set the parameter θ to range from 0 to 2π in steps of 0.05. The graph shows the 12-petaled rose produced by the equation $r = 2 \sin 6\theta$. As you can see, the term "rose" was chosen by mathematicians, not by botanists.

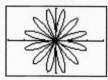

$[-3, 3]$ by $[-2, 2]$

2. Graph $r = 2 \sin n\theta$ for various positive integer values of n until you can state a rule for how n determines the number of petals in the rose. What is the rule?

3. At first glance it appears that the petal behavior is quite different for odd and even values of n, but if you watch the grapher carefully you will see that there is a consistent rule for the "number of petals traced" in each case. Explain.

4. Use NINT to find the total area enclosed by the petals of $r = 2 \sin 2\theta$. Over what θ-interval did you integrate? Why?

5. The NINT answer is approximate. Can you make an educated guess at what the exact area might be?

6. Repeat step 4 for the function $r = 2 \sin 6\theta$. How does the number of petals compare to the rose in step 4? How do the areas of the two roses compare?

7. Repeat step 4 for the function $r = 2 \sin 3\theta$. Did you still integrate over the same interval? Why or why not?

8. Make a conjecture about the area of the rose generated by $r = 2 \sin n\theta$ for an arbitrary positive integer n. Do you need a separate rule for odd and even values of n? Explain.

9. Show that the area of a single petal of $r = 2 \sin n\theta$ is $2 \int_0^{\pi/n} \sin^2 (n\theta) \, d\theta$, regardless of the value of n.

10. Use substitution to show that the integral in step 9 equals $\dfrac{2}{n} \int_0^{\pi} \sin^2 (u) \, du$.

11. If $2 \int_0^{\pi} \sin^2 (u) \, du = A$, explain why steps 2 and 10 enable us to conclude that the area of the rose generated by $r = 2 \sin (n\theta)$ will be the same number A for any odd value of n and that it will be $2A$ for any even value of n.

12. Find A and write the general rule for the area of the rose generated by $r = 2 \sin (n\theta)$ for any positive integer n. Was your conjecture correct in step 8?

Sample Tests for The Advanced Placement Examinations

The Advanced Placement Calculus Examinations are three hours long and evaluate how well students have mastered the concepts and techniques in either the AB or BC Calculus course. Each examination consists of (1) a multiple-choice section that tests proficiency over a broad spectrum of topics and (2) a problem section that requires students to demonstrate their ability in solving problems requiring a more extensive chain of reasoning.

As of May 1998, the examination will be based on the new Advanced Placement Course Description. In Part A of the multiple-choice section (28 questions completed in 50 minutes), students will **not** be allowed to use calculators. Part B of the multiple-choice section (17 questions in 40 minutes) includes some questions for which a graphing calculator **is required** and some where students will have to decide whether a graphing calculator is appropriate.

The problem section (6 questions completed in 90 minutes) is designed to utilize the graphing calculator for some problems.

Both the multiple-choice and free-response sections are given equal weight in determining the grade for the examination.

The following tests are intended to give students practice with the type of exam they will take. You may wish to simulate the conditions of the exam, providing the exact amount of time for each section and using the multiple choice answer section that is provided.

Advanced Placement Calculus AB test

Section I—Part A (55 minutes)

Choose the best answer for each question. Your score is determined by subtracting one-fourth of the number of wrong answers from the number of correct answers. **Calculators are not permitted.**

1.

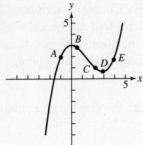

For the graph shown, at which point is it true that $\dfrac{dy}{dx} < 0$ and $\dfrac{d^2y}{dx^2} > 0$?

(A) A (B) B (C) C (D) D (E) E

2. Find the area of the region bounded by the x-axis and the graph of $y = (x + 1)(x - 2)^2$.

(A) 1.25   (B) 2.75   (C) 5.25   (D) 6.25   (E) 6.75

3. Which of the following is an antiderivative of $x^2 \sec^2 x^3$?

(A) $2x \sec^2 x^3 + 6x^4 \sec^2 x^3 \tan x^3$

(B) $2x \sec^2 x^3 + 6x^3 \sec x^3$

(C) $\dfrac{1}{3} \tan x^3 - 5$

(D) $3 \tan x^3 + \pi$

(E) $-\dfrac{1}{3} \cot x^3 + 4$

4. Line L is normal to the curve defined by $2xy^2 - 3y = 18$ at the point $(3, 2)$. The slope of line L is

(A) $\dfrac{21}{8}$ (B) $\dfrac{32}{3}$ (C) $-\dfrac{10}{21}$ (D) $\dfrac{8}{21}$ (E) $-\dfrac{8}{21}$

5.

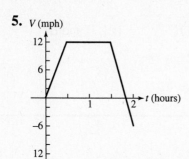

A bicyclist rides along a straight road starting from home at $t = 0$. The graph above shows the bicyclist's velocity as a function of t. How far from home is the bicyclist after 2 hours?

(A) 13 miles (B) 16.5 miles (C) 17.5 miles (D) 18 miles (E) 20 miles

---

6. Find the value of x at which the graph of $y = \dfrac{1}{x} + \sqrt{x}$ has a point of inflection.

(A) 2 (B) $4^{2/3}$ (C) 4 (D) 6 (E) 8

---

7. Find $\lim\limits_{x \to \infty} \dfrac{3x + 2x^3}{3x^3 - 4x^2 + 2x}$.

(A) $\dfrac{2}{3}$ (B) $\dfrac{3}{2}$ (C) 1 (D) $-\dfrac{1}{2}$ (E) $-\dfrac{3}{4}$

8. Let y be a differentiable function with $\dfrac{dy}{dx} > 0$ for all x. For which of the following values of y is it true that $\dfrac{d}{dx}y^2 = 8\dfrac{d}{dx}\ln y$?

   I. $y = \dfrac{1}{2}$

   II. $y = 2$

   III. $y = 4$

(A) I only   (B) II only   (C) III only   (D) I and II   (E) II and III

9.

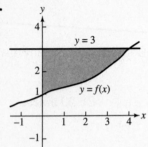

Assume that $f(x)$ is a one-to-one function. The area of the shaded region is equal to which of the following definite integrals?

   I. $\displaystyle\int_0^4 [f(x) - 3]\, dx$

   II. $\displaystyle\int_4^0 [f(x) - 3]\, dx$

   III. $\displaystyle\int_1^3 f^{-1}(y)\, dy$

(A) I only   (B) II only   (C) III only   (D) I and III   (E) II and III

---

10. Let $f(x) = \cos(3\pi x^2)$. Find $f'\left(\dfrac{1}{3}\right)$.

(A) $-\sqrt{3}\pi$ (B) $\sqrt{3}\pi$ (C) 0 (D) $-\dfrac{\sqrt{3}\pi}{2}$ (E) $-\pi$

11.

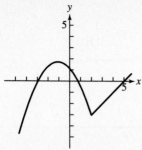

The graph of a function $y = f(x)$ is shown above. Which of the following are true for the function f?

I. $f'(2)$ is defined.

II. $\lim\limits_{x \to 2^+} f(x) = \lim\limits_{x \to 2^-} f(x)$

III. $f'(x) < 0$ for all x in the open interval $(-1, 2)$.

(A) I only   (B) II only   (C) III only   (D) II and III   (E) I, II, and III

---

12. Let $f(x) = \tan^{-1} x$. Find $f'(2)$.

(A) $\dfrac{\pi}{3}$ (B) $\dfrac{1}{5}$ (C) $\dfrac{1}{2}$ (D) $\dfrac{1}{2\sqrt{3}}$ (E) Undefined

---

13. Evaluate $\displaystyle\int (\cos x - e^{2x})\, dx$.

(A) $-\sin x - \dfrac{1}{2}e^{2x} + C$

(B) $\sin x - \dfrac{1}{2}e^{2x} + C$

(C) $-\sin x - 2e^{2x} + C$

(D) $\sin x - 2e^{2x} + C$

(E) $-\cos x - \dfrac{1}{2}e^{2x} + C$

14. Let $f(x) = e^{x^3 - 2x^2 - 4x + 5}$. Then f has a local minimum at $x =$

(A) -2 　　　　(B) $-\dfrac{2}{3}$ 　　　　(C) $\dfrac{2}{3}$ 　　　　(D) 1 　　　　(E) 2

---

15. The acceleration of a particle moving along the x-axis is $a(t) = 12t - 10$.
At $t = 0$, the velocity is 3.
At $t = 1$, the position is $x = 4$.
Find the position at $t = 2$.

(A) 2 　　　　(B) 4 　　　　(C) 5 　　　　(D) 6 　　　　(E) 7

---

16. Let f be differentiable for all real numbers. Which of the following must be true for any real numbers a and b?

I. $\displaystyle \int_{2}^{a} f(x)\, dx = \int_{2}^{b} f(x)\, dx + \int_{b}^{a} f(x)\, dx$

II. $\displaystyle \int_{a}^{b} 3 f(x)\, dx = 3 \int_{a}^{b} f(x)\, dx$

III. $\displaystyle \int_{a}^{b} \left([f(x)]^2 + f'(x) \right) dx = [f(b)]^2 - [f(a)]^2$

(A) I only 　　　(B) II only 　　　(C) I and II 　　　(D) II and III 　　　(E) I, II, and III

---

17. Find an equation of the line tangent to the graph of $y = \dfrac{3x}{x^2 - 6}$ at $x = 3$.

(A) $5x + y = 18$ 　　(B) $5x - y = 12$ 　　(C) $5x + 3y = 24$ 　　(D) $x - 5y = -12$ 　　(E) $x + y = 6$

18. Let $g(x) = \lim\limits_{h \to 0} \dfrac{(x+h)^2 - x^2}{h}$. For what value of x does $g(x) = 2$?

(A) $x = 1$ (B) $x = 2$ (C) $x = 3$ (D) $x = 4$ (E) $x = 5$

---

19. Let f be a differentiable function of x that satisfies $f(1) = 7$ and $f(4) = 3$. Which of the following conditions would guarantee that the tangent line at $x = c$ is parallel to the secant line joining $(1, f(1))$ to $(4, f(4))$?

(A) $f(c) = \dfrac{3}{2}$ (B) $f(c) = 5$ (C) $f'(c) = -\dfrac{3}{4}$ (D) $f'(c) = -\dfrac{4}{3}$ (E) $f'(c) = \dfrac{4}{3}$

---

20. Let $f(x) = x^3 - 12x$. Which statement about this function is false?

(A) The function has one inflection point.

(B) The function is concave upward for $x > 0$.

(C) The function has two relative extrema.

(D) The function is increasing for values of x between -2 and 2.

(E) The function has a relative minimum at $x = 2$.

---

21. $\displaystyle\int_{2}^{3} 8x(x^2 - 5)\, dx =$

(A) $\dfrac{74}{3}$ (B) 30 (C) 90 (D) 112 (E) $\dfrac{370}{3}$

---

22. Let $f(x) = \dfrac{d}{dx}\displaystyle\int_{0}^{x} \sqrt{t^2 + 16}\, dt$. What is $f(-3)$?

(A) -5 (B) -4 (C) 3 (D) 4 (E) 5

---

23. If $\frac{dy}{dx} = xy^2$ and $y = -\frac{1}{3}$ when $x = 2$, what is y when $x = 4$?

(A) $-\frac{1}{3}$ (B) $-\frac{1}{5}$ (C) $-\frac{1}{9}$ (D) $\frac{1}{3}$ (E) $\frac{1}{9}$

---

24. Use the Trapezoidal Rule with $n = 3$ to approximate the area between the curve $y = x^2$ and the x-axis for $1 \le x \le 4$.

(A) 14   (B) 21   (C) 21.5   (D) 29   (E) 30

---

25. Let $f(x)$ be a continuous function that is defined for all real numbers x.
If $f(x) = \frac{x^2 - x - 6}{x^2 - 5x + 6}$ when $x^2 - 5x + 6 \ne 0$, what is $f(3)$?

(A) 0   (B) 1   (C) 2   (D) 4   (E) 5

---

26. Find the derivative of $\cos^3 2x$.
   (A) $-\sin^3 2x$
   (B) $6 \cos^2 2x$
   (C) $6 \cos^2 2x \sin 2x$
   (D) $-3 \cos^2 2x \sin 2x$
   (E) $-6 \cos^2 2x \sin 2x$

---

27. Let f be a twice-differentiable function whose derivative $f'(x)$ is increasing for all x. Which of the following must be true for all x?

    I. $f(x) > 0$

    II. $f'(x) > 0$

    III. $f''(x) > 0$

(A) I only   (B) II only   (C) III only   (D) I and II   (E) II and III

---

28. The function $f(x) = x^3 - 6x^2 + 9x - 4$ has a local maximum at

(A) $x = 0$ (B) $x = 1$ (C) $x = 2$ (D) $x = 3$ (E) $x = 4$

Choose the *best* answer for each question. (If the exact answer does not appear among the choices, choose the best approximation for the exact answer.) Your score is determined by subtracting one-fourth of the number of wrong answers from the number of correct answers. **You may use a graphing calculator.**

29. The velocity of a particle moving along a straight line is given by $v(t) = 3x^2 - 4x$. Find an expression for the acceleration of the particle.

(A) $3x - 4$ (B) $6x - 4$ (C) $x^3 - 4$ (D) $x^3 - 2x^2$ (E) $3x^2 - 4$

30. Find the average value of the function $y = x^3 - 4x$ on the closed interval $[0, 4]$.

(A) 8 (B) 12 (C) 24 (D) 32 (E) 48

31. A region is enclosed by the x-axis and the graph of the parabola $y = 9 - x^2$. Find the volume of the solid generated when this region is revolved about the x-axis.

(A) 36π (B) 40.5π (C) 129.6π (D) 194.4π (E) 259.2π

32. Which of the following is an antiderivative of $x\sqrt{x^2 + 3}$?

(A) $\frac{1}{3}x^{3/2}$ (B) $\frac{1}{3}x^3$ (C) $\frac{1}{3}(x^2 + 3)^{3/2}$ (D) $\frac{2}{3}(x^2 + 3)^{3/2}$ (E) $(x^2 + 3)^{3/2}$

33. Which of the following functions has the fastest rate of growth as $x \to \infty$?

(A) $y = x^{18} - 5x$ (B) $y = 5x^2$ (C) $y = \ln x^2$ (D) $y = (\ln x)^2$ (E) $y = e^{0.01x}$

34.

x	3.3	3.4	3.5	3.6	3.7
$f(x)$	3.69	3.96	4.25	4.56	4.89

Let f be a differentiable function that is defined for all real numbers x. Use the table above to estimate $f'(3.5)$.

(A) 0.3   (B) 1.8   (C) 2.7   (D) 3.0   (E) 6.0

---

35. The weight in pounds of a certain bear cub t months after birth is given by $w(t)$. If $w(2) = 36$, $w(7) = 84$, and $\frac{dw}{dt}$ was proportional to the cub's weight for the first 15 months of his life, how much did the cub weigh when he was 11 months old?

(A) 125 pounds   (B) 135 pounds   (C) 145 pounds   (D) 155 pounds   (E) 165 pounds

---

36. Let $f(x) = \begin{cases} 3x^2 - 4, & \text{for } x \leq 1 \\ 6x - 5, & \text{for } x > 1 \end{cases}$.

Which of the following are true statements about this function?

     I. $\lim\limits_{x \to 1} f(x)$ exists.

     II. $\lim\limits_{x \to 1} f'(x)$ exists.

     III. $f'(1)$ exists.

(A) None   (B) II only   (C) III only   (D) II and III   (E) I, II, and III

---

37. Two particles are moving along the x-axis. Their positions are given by $x_1(t) = 2t^2 - 5t + 7$ and $x_2(t) = \sin 2t$, respectively. If $a_1(t)$ and $a_2(t)$ represent the acceleration functions of the particles, find the numbers of values of t in the closed interval $[0, 5]$ for which $a_1(t) = a_2(t)$.

(A) 0   (B) 1   (C) 2   (D) 3   (E) 4 or more

38. The function $f(x) = e^x - x^3$ has how many critical points?

(A) 0   (B) 1   (C) 2   (D) 3   (E) 4 or more

---

39. A dog heading due north at a constant speed of 2 meters per second trots past a fire hydrant at $t = 0$ sec. Another dog heading due east at a constant speed of 3 meters per second trots by the hydrant at $t = 1$ sec. At $t = 9$ sec, the rate of change of the distance between the two dogs is

(A) 3.2 m/sec   (B) 3.6 m/sec   (C) 4.0 m/sec   (D) 4.4 m/sec   (E) 4.8 m/sec

---

40. Suppose air is pumped into a balloon at a rate given by $r(t) = \dfrac{(\ln t)^2}{t}$ ft^3/sec for $t \geq 1$ sec. If the volume of the balloon is 1.3 ft^3 at $t = 1$ sec, what is the volume of the balloon at $t = 5$ sec?

(A) 2.7 ft^3 (B) 3.0 ft^3 (C) 3.3 ft^3 (D) 3.6 ft^3 (E) 3.9 ft^3

---

41. Suppose f and g are even functions that are continuous for all x, and let a be a real number. Which of the following expressions must have the same value?

I. $\displaystyle\int_{-a}^{a} [f(x) + g(x)]\, dx$

II. $\displaystyle 2\int_{0}^{a} [f(x) + g(x)]\, dx$

III. $\displaystyle\int_{-a}^{a} f(x)\, dx + \int_{-a}^{a} g(x)\, dx$

(A) I and II only   (B) I and III only   (C) II and III only   (D) I, II, and III   (E) None

---

42. Let $f(x) = x^5 + x$. Find the value of $\dfrac{d}{dx} f^{-1}(x)$ at $x = 2$.

(A) $-\dfrac{1}{6}$ (B) $\dfrac{1}{6}$ (C) $\dfrac{1}{81}$ (D) 6   (E) 81

43. Find the approximate value of x where $f(x) = x^2 - 3\sqrt{x+2}$ has its absolute minimum.

(A) -4.5 (B) -2 (C) 0   (D) 0.5   (E) 2.5

44.

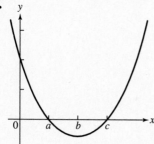

The graph of $y = f'(x)$ is shown. Which of the following statements about the function $f(x)$ are true?

  I. $f(x)$ is decreasing for all x between a and c.

 II. The graph of f is concave up for all x between a and c.

III. $f(x)$ has a relative minimum at $x = a$.

(A) I only   (B) II only   (C) III only   (D) I and III   (E) I, II, and III

45. Let $f(x) = g(h(x))$, where $h(2) = 3$, $h'(2) = 4$, $g(3) = 2$, and $g'(3) = 5$. Find $f'(2)$.
  (A) 6
  (B) 8
  (C) 15
  (D) 20
  (E) More information is needed to find $f'(2)$.

Section II (90 minutes)

Show your work. In order to receive full credit, you must show enough detail to demonstrate a clear understanding of the concepts involved. You may use a graphing calculator. Where appropriate, you may give numerical answers in exact form or as decimal approximations correct to three decimal places.

1. Let $f(x) = \ln(-x^2 + x + 6)$.

    (a) Find the domain of f.

    (b) Sketch the graph of f in the viewing window shown.

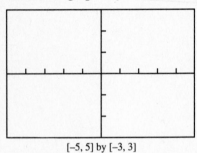

               [–5, 5] by [–3, 3]

    (c) Find the equation of each horizontal or vertical asymptote of the graph of f.

    (d) Find $f'(x)$.

    (e) Find the range of f. Use $f'(x)$ to justify your answer.

2. For $t \geq 0$, a particle moves along the x-axis with a velocity given by $v(t) = 2t - 5 \sin \pi t$. At $t = 0$, the particle is located at $x = 0$.

    (a) Write an expression for the acceleration $a(t)$ of the particle.

    (b) Write an expression for the position $x(t)$ of the particle.

    (c) For what values of t ($t \geq 0$) is the particle moving to the left?

    (d) For $t > 1$, find the position of the particle the first time the velocity of the particle is zero.

3.

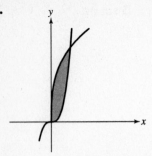

The shaded region is enclosed by the graphs of $y = x^3$ and $y = 4\sqrt[3]{4x}$.

(a) Find the coordinates of the point in the first quadrant where the two curves intersect.

(b) Use an integral with respect to x to find the area of the shaded region.

(c) Set up an integral with respect to y that could be used to find the area of the shaded region.

(d) Without using absolute values, write an integral expression that gives the volume of the solid generated by revolving the shaded region about the line $x = -1$. Do not evaluate.

4.

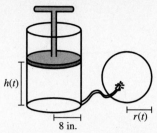

The figure above shows a pump connected by a flexible tube to a spherical balloon. The pump consists of a cylindrical container of radius 8 inches, with a piston that moves up and down according to the equation $h(t) = \dfrac{24}{t+1} + \ln(t+1)$ for $0 \le t \le 100$, where t is measured in seconds and $h(t)$ is measured in inches. As the piston moves up and down, the total volume of air enclosed in the pump and the balloon remains constant, and $r(t) = 0$ at $t = 0$. $\left(\text{The volume of a sphere with radius } r \text{ is } \dfrac{4}{3}\pi r^3. \right)$

(a) Write an expression in terms of $h(t)$ and $r(t)$ for the total volume of the air enclosed in the pump and the balloon. (Do not include the air in the flexible tube.)

(b) Find the minimum volume of air in the pump and when it occurs.

(c) Find the rate of change of the volume of the air enclosed in the pump at $t = 3$ sec.

(d) At $t = 3$ sec, find the radius of the balloon and the rate of change of the radius of the balloon.

5. A function $y = f(x)$ is defined by $5\sqrt{x} + xy + y^3 = 11$.

(a) Find an expression for $f'(x) = \dfrac{dy}{dx}$ in terms of x and y.

(b) Find the equation of the line that is tangent to the graph of $y = f(x)$ at the point $(0.25, 2)$.

(c) Use the tangent line from part (b) to estimate $f(0.6)$.

(d) Write an equation whose solution is the exact value of $f(0.6)$.
To the nearest thousandth, what is $f(0.6)$?

(e) Would it be appropriate to use the tangent line from part (b) to estimate $f(-0.1)$? Explain.

6.

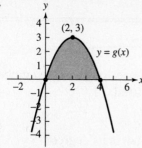

The graph of a differentiable function g is shown. The area of the shaded region is 8 square units. Let f be a differentiable function such that $f(0) = -3$ and $f'(x) = g(x)$ for $-1 \leq x \leq 5$.

(a) Find $f(4)$.

_____

(b) For what values of x is the graph of $y = f(x)$ concave upward? Explain.

_____

(c) Write an expression for $f(x)$. Your answer should involve a definite integral and should be expressed in terms of the function g.

_____

(d) Sketch a possible graph for $y = f(x)$.

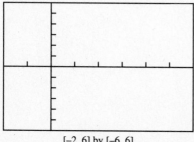

[-2, 6] by [-6, 6]

Section I—Part A (55 minutes)

Choose the best answer for each question. Your score is determined by subtracting one-fourth of the number of wrong answers from the number of correct answers. **Calculators are not permitted.**

---

1. Let $p(x) = \int_0^x (12t^3 + 6t^2 + 4t + 2)\, dt$. If $p(x)$ is expressed as a polynomial, what is its degree?

(A) 0   (B) 1   (C) 2   (D) 3   (E) 4

---

2. Evaluate $\int x \cos 2x\, dx$.

(A) $\dfrac{1}{2}x \cos 2x - \dfrac{1}{4} \sin 2x + C$

(B) $\dfrac{1}{2}x \sin 2x - \dfrac{1}{4} \cos 2x + C$

(C) $\dfrac{1}{2}x \sin 2x - \dfrac{1}{4} \sin 2x + C$

(D) $\dfrac{1}{2}x \cos 2x + \dfrac{1}{4} \sin 2x + C$

(E) $\dfrac{1}{2}x \sin 2x + \dfrac{1}{4} \cos 2x + C$

---

3. Which of the following is a term in the Taylor series about $x = 0$ for the function $f(x) = \cos 2x$?

(A) $-\dfrac{1}{2}x^2$ (B) $-\dfrac{4}{3}x^3$ (C) $\dfrac{2}{3}x^4$ (D) $\dfrac{1}{60}x^5$ (E) $\dfrac{4}{45}x^6$

---

4. If $\dfrac{dy}{dx} = (x + 3)e^{-2y}$, then which of the following is a possible expression for y?

(A) $\dfrac{1}{2} \ln (x^2 + 6x + 5)$

(B) $\ln (x^2 + 6x - 4)$

(C) $\dfrac{1}{2} \ln (x^2 + 6x) - 3$

(D) $\dfrac{1}{2} \ln \left(\dfrac{1}{4}x^2 + \dfrac{3}{2}x\right)$

(E) $\dfrac{1}{2} \ln (x^2 + 3x)$

---

5. Let $f(x) = \begin{cases} 2x - 5, & \text{for } x \le 3 \\ \sqrt{x + 1}, & \text{for } x > 3 \end{cases}$.

Find $\displaystyle\int_0^8 f(x)\, dx$.

(A) 24
(B) $\dfrac{45}{2}$
(C) $\dfrac{52}{3}$
(D) $\dfrac{32}{3}\sqrt{2} - 2\sqrt{3}$
(E) $\dfrac{20}{3}$

---

6. The line tangent to the graph of $y = x^3 - 3x^2 - 2x + 1$ at $x = -1$ will also intersect the curve at which of the following values of x?

(A) $x = 4$
(B) $x = 5$
(C) $x = 6$
(D) $x = 7$
(E) $x = 8$

---

7. $\displaystyle\lim_{h \to 0} \dfrac{\tan\left(\dfrac{\pi}{4} + h\right) - \tan\dfrac{\pi}{4}}{h} =$

(A) $\dfrac{1}{2}$
(B) $\dfrac{\sqrt{2}}{2}$
(C) 1
(D) $\sqrt{2}$
(E) 2

8. A curve in the xy-plane is defined by the parametric equations $x = t^3 + 2$ and $y = t^2 - 5t$. Find the slope of the line tangent to the curve at the point where $x = 10$.

(A) -12 (B) $-\dfrac{3}{5}$ (C) $-\dfrac{1}{8}$ (D) $-\dfrac{1}{12}$ (E) $\dfrac{1}{20}$

---

9. Assume that $g'(x) = h(x)$ and $f(x) = x^2$. Which of the following expressions is equal to $\dfrac{d}{dx} f(g(x))$?

(A) $2x\, g(x)$ (B) $2x\, h(x)$ (C) $2\, g(x)\, h(x)$ (D) $f'(x)\, g(x)\, h(x)$ (E) $x^2 h(x) + 2x\, g(x)$

---

10. Let $f(x) = \begin{cases} 2x, & \text{for } x < 1 \\ 2x - 3, & \text{for } x \geq 1 \end{cases}$.

Let $g(x) = \ln\left[(x - 1)^2\right]$.

Which of the following functions are continuous at $x = 1$?

I. $f'(x)$

II. $\displaystyle\int_0^x f(t)\, dt$

III. $g(x)$

(A) I only   (B) II only   (C) III only   (D) I and II   (E) I and III

11.

Which of the following differential equations could be represented by the slope field shown above?

(A) $\dfrac{dy}{dx} = -x^3 + 4x$

(B) $\dfrac{dy}{dx} = x^2 - 2$

(C) $\dfrac{dy}{dx} = \sin x$

(D) $\dfrac{dy}{dx} = -\sin x$

(E) $\dfrac{dy}{dx} = \cos x$

---

12. A particle is moving along the x-axis according to the equation $x(t) = 4t^2 - \sin 3t$ where x is given in feet and t is given in seconds. Find the acceleration at $t = \dfrac{\pi}{2}$.

(A) -1 ft/sec^2 (B) 5 ft/sec^2 (C) 11 ft/sec^2 (D) 17 ft/sec^2 (E) 2π ft/sec^2

---

13. Find the values of x for which the series $\displaystyle\sum_{n=1}^{\infty} \dfrac{(x-2)^n}{n(-3)^n}$ converges.

(A) $x = 2$ only

(B) $-1 \le x < 5$

(C) $-1 < x \le 5$

(D) $-1 < x < 5$

(E) All real numbers

---

14. The position vector of a particle moving in the xy-plane is given by $\mathbf{r}(t) = \langle \sin^{-1} t, (t + 4)^2 \rangle$ for $-1 \le t \le 1$. The velocity vector at $t = 0.6$ is

(A) $\langle \sin^{-1} 0.6, 21.16 \rangle$

(B) $\langle 1.25, 9.2 \rangle$

(C) $\left\langle \dfrac{5}{3}, 1.2 \right\rangle$

(D) $\left\langle \dfrac{5}{3}, 9.2 \right\rangle$

(E) $\left\langle \dfrac{75}{64}, 2 \right\rangle$

---

15. Evaluate $\displaystyle\int_2^\infty x e^{-x^2}\, dx$.

(A) $\dfrac{1}{2}e^{-2}$ (B) $-\dfrac{1}{2}e^{-2}$ (C) $\dfrac{1}{2}e^{-4}$ (D) $-\dfrac{1}{2}e^{-4}$ (E) ∞

---

16. Let f and g be functions that are differentiable for all real numbers, with $\lim\limits_{x \to 0} f(x) = 3$ and $\lim\limits_{x \to 0} g(x) = 5$. Which of the following must be equal to $\lim\limits_{x \to 0} \dfrac{f(x)}{g(x)}$? $\left(\text{You may assume that } \lim\limits_{x \to 0} \dfrac{f(x)}{g(x)} \text{ exists.}\right)$

I. $\dfrac{3}{5}$

II. $\dfrac{f(0)}{g(0)}$

III. $\lim\limits_{x \to 0} \dfrac{f'(0)}{g'(0)}$

(A) None (B) I and II (C) I and III (D) II and III (E) I, II, and III

17. Let $f(x) = \sum_{n=1}^{\infty} (\cos x)^{3n}$. Evaluate $f\left(\dfrac{2\pi}{3}\right)$.

(A) $-\dfrac{1}{7}$

(B) $-\dfrac{1}{9}$

(C) $\dfrac{1}{7}$

(D) $\dfrac{8}{9}$

(E) The series diverges.

---

18. Let $f(x) = \displaystyle\int_{0}^{2x} e^{t^2+5}\, dt$. Find $f'(x)$.

(A) e^{x^2+5} (B) e^{4x^2+5} (C) $2e^{x^2+5}$ (D) $2e^{4x^2+5}$ (E) $4e^{x^2+5}$

---

19. A particle is moving along the graph of the curve $y = \ln(4x + 3)$. At the instant when the particle crosses the y-axis, the y-coordinate of its location is changing at the rate of 12 units per second. Find the rate of change of the x-coordinate of the particle's location.

(A) 4 units per second

(B) 9 units per second

(C) 16 units per second

(D) 36 units per second

(E) 4 ln 3 units per second

---

20. Find $\displaystyle\lim_{x\to\infty} \left(\dfrac{2x+1}{2x}\right)^{3x}$

(A) 1.5 (B) 6 (C) $e^{1.5}$ (D) e^{6} (E) ∞

---

21. Use implicit differentiation to find $\dfrac{dy}{dx}$ for the equation $e^{xy} + 4y = 7$.

(A) $-\dfrac{1}{4}e^{xy}$

(B) $\dfrac{y}{x + 4e^{-xy}}$

(C) $\dfrac{7 - ye^{xy}}{4 + xe^{xy}}$

(D) $-\dfrac{y}{4}e^{xy}$

(E) $-\dfrac{ye^{xy}}{xe^{xy} + 4}$

---

22. Which of the following is equal to $\displaystyle\int_1^3 (2x^2 - 5)^3 x\, dx$?

(A) $\dfrac{1}{4}\displaystyle\int_1^3 u^3\, du$

(B) $\dfrac{1}{4}\displaystyle\int_{-3}^{13} u^3\, du$

(C) $\displaystyle\int_{-3}^{13} u^3\, du$

(D) $4\displaystyle\int_1^3 u^3\, du$

(E) $4\displaystyle\int_{-3}^{13} u^3\, du$

---

23. Find the area of the region above the x-axis and beneath one arch of the graph of $y = \dfrac{1}{2} + \sin x$.

(A) $\dfrac{2\pi}{3} + \sqrt{3}$

(B) $\dfrac{2\pi}{3} + 1$

(C) $\sqrt{3} - \dfrac{\pi}{3}$

(D) $\sqrt{3} + \dfrac{4\pi}{3}$

(E) $\dfrac{7\pi}{12} + \dfrac{\sqrt{3}}{2} + 1$

---

24. A curve is defined parametrically by $x = t^3 - 5$ and $y = e^{2t}$ for $0 \le t \le 4$.
Which of the following is equal to the length of the curve?

(A) $\displaystyle\int_0^4 \sqrt{(t^3 - 5)^2 + e^{4t}}\, dt$

(B) $2\pi\displaystyle\int_0^4 (t^3 - 5)\sqrt{9t^4 + 4e^{4t}}\, dt$

(C) $\displaystyle\int_0^4 \sqrt{9t^4 + 4e^{4t}}\, dt$

(D) $\displaystyle\int_0^4 \sqrt{6t^2 e^{2t} + 1}\, dt$

(E) $2\displaystyle\int_0^4 \sqrt{t^4 + e^{4t}}\, dt$

---

25. Find the values of x for which the graph of $y = xe^x$ is concave downward.

    (A) $x < -2$ (B) $x > -2$ (C) $x < -1$ (D) $x > -1$ (E) $x < 0$

---

26. The graph of $f(x) = x^3 + x^2$ has a point of inflection at

    (A) $x = \dfrac{1}{3}$ (B) $x = -\dfrac{1}{3}$ (C) $x = -\dfrac{2}{3}$ (D) $x = \dfrac{2}{27}$ (E) $x = 0$

---

27. Use partial fractions to evaluate $\displaystyle\int_3^5 \frac{4x - 9}{2x^2 - 9x + 10}\, dx$

    (A) $\ln 3 + \ln 5$ (B) $2 \ln 3 + \ln 5$ (C) $\ln 3 + 2 \ln 5$ (D) $\ln 5 - \ln 3$ (E) $2 \ln 5 - \ln 3$

---

28. Find the sum of the geometric series $\dfrac{9}{8} - \dfrac{3}{4} + \dfrac{1}{2} - \dfrac{1}{3} + \cdots$

    (A) $\dfrac{3}{5}$ (B) $\dfrac{5}{8}$ (C) $\dfrac{13}{24}$ (D) $\dfrac{27}{8}$ (E) $\dfrac{27}{40}$

Choose the *best* answer for each question. (If the exact answer does not appear among the choices, choose the best approximation for the exact answer.) Your score is determined by subtracting one-fourth of the number of wrong answers from the number of correct answers. **You may use a graphing calculator.**

29. Find the average value of the function $y = x\sqrt{\cos x}$ on the closed interval $[5, 7]$.

(A) 4.4   (B) 5.4   (C) 6.4   (D) 7.4   (E) 10.8

30. The series $x + x^3 + \dfrac{x^5}{2!} + \dfrac{x^7}{3!} + \cdots + \dfrac{x^{2n+1}}{n!} + \cdots$ is the Maclaurin series for

(A) $x \ln (1 + x^2)$ (B) $x \ln (1 - x^2)$ (C) e^{x^2} (D) xe^{x^2} (E) $x^2 e^x$

31. A region is enclosed by the graphs of the line $y = 2$ and the parabola $y = 6 - x^2$. Find the volume of the solid generated when this region is revolved about the x-axis.

(A) 76.8   (B) 107.2   (C) 167.6   (D) 183.3   (E) 241.3

32. Find the area, in terms of k, for the region enclosed by the graphs of $y = x^4$ and $y = k$. (Assume $k > 0$.)

(A) $(2 + k)\sqrt[4]{k}$ (B) $2k\left(k - \dfrac{k^2}{5}\right)$ (C) $2(1 + k)\sqrt[4]{k}$ (D) $1.6k^{5/4}$ (E) $1.8k^{5/4}$

33. The area enclosed by the graph of $r = 5 \cos 4\theta$ is

(A) 5   (B) 10   (C) 6.25π (D) 12.5π (E) 25π

34. Let $f(x)$ be a differentiable function whose domain is the closed interval $[0, 5]$, and let $F(x) = \int_0^x f(t)\, dt$. If $F(5) = 10$, which of the following must be true?

   I. $F(x) = 2$ for some value of x in $[0, 5]$.

   II. $f(x) = 2$ for some value of x in $[0, 5]$.

   III. $f'(x) = 2$ for some value of x in $[0, 5]$.

(A) I only   (B) II only   (C) III only   (D) I and II   (E) I, II, and III

---

35. The velocity of a particle moving along the x-axis is given by $v(t) = t \sin t^2$. Find the total distance traveled from $t = 0$ to $t = 3$.

(A) 1.0   (B) 1.5   (C) 2.0   (D) 2.5   (E) 3.0

36.

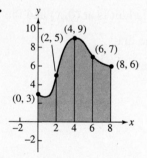

Use the Trapezoidal Rule with the indicated subintervals to estimate the area of the shaded region.

(A) 48   (B) 50   (C) 51   (D) 52   (E) 54

37. Let $g(x) = \int_0^x (t + 2)(t - 3)e^{-t}\, dt$.

For what values of x is g decreasing?

(A) $x < -1.49$

(B) $x > 0.37$

(C) $-2 < x < 3$

(D) $x < -2.72, x > 0$

(E) Nowhere

38.

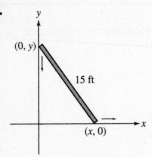

A 15-foot ladder is leaning against a building as shown, so that the top of the ladder is at $(0, y)$ and the bottom is at $(x, 0)$. The ladder is falling because the ground is slippery; assume that $\dfrac{dy}{dt} = -12$ feet per second at the instant when $x = 9$ feet. Find $\dfrac{dx}{dt}$ at this instant.

(A) 6 feet per second

(B) 9 feet per second

(C) 12 feet per second

(D) 16 feet per second

(E) 20 feet per second

---

39. The infinite region beneath the curve $y = \dfrac{5}{x + 1}$ in the first quadrant is revolved about the x-axis to generate a solid. The volume of this solid is

(A) 5   (B) 5π (C) 25   (D) 25π (E) ∞

---

40. Let $f(t) = \sin t - 2 \cos t^2$, where $0 \le t \le 4$. For what value of t is $f(t)$ increasing most rapidly?

(A) 1.76   (B) 2.81   (C) 3.32   (D) 3.56   (E) 3.77

41.

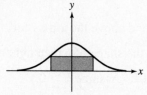

A rectangle is inscribed under the curve $y = e^{-x^2}$ as shown above. Find the maximum possible area of the rectangle.

(A) 0.43   (B) 0.61   (C) 0.71   (D) 0.86   (E) 1.77

---

42. Let $f_n(x)$ denote the nth-order Taylor polynomial at $x = 0$ for $\cos x$ (that is, the sum of the terms up to and including the x^n term). For what values of n is $f_n(0.8) < \cos x$?

(A) 0, 2, 4, 6, 8, 10, ...
(B) 1, 3, 5, 7, 9, 11, ...
(C) 1, 2, 5, 6, 9, 10, ...
(D) 2, 3, 6, 7, 10, 11, ...
(E) 3, 4, 7, 8, 11, 12, ...

---

43. Find the average rate of change of y with respect to x on the closed interval $[0, 3]$ if $\dfrac{dy}{dx} = \dfrac{x}{x^2 + 1}$.

(A) $\dfrac{1}{6} \ln 10$ (B) $\dfrac{1}{6} \ln 3$ (C) $\dfrac{1}{2} \ln 10$ (D) $\dfrac{1}{10}$ (E) $\dfrac{3}{10}$

---

44. If the derivative of f is $f' = x(x-1)^2(x-2)^3(x-3)^4$, find the number of points where f has a local maximum.

(A) None   (B) One   (C) Two   (D) Three   (E) Four

---

45. The base of a solid is the region in the xy-plane beneath the curve $y = \sin kx$ and above the x-axis for $0 \le x \le \dfrac{\pi}{2k}$. Each of the solid's cross-sections perpendicular to the x-axis has the shape of a rectangle with height $\cos^2 kx$. If the volume of the solid is 1 cubic unit, find the value of k. (Assume $k > 0$.)

(A) 3   (B) 3π (C) $\dfrac{1}{3\pi}$ (D) $\dfrac{\pi}{3}$ (E) $\dfrac{1}{3}$

Advanced Placement Calculus BC test

Section II (90 minutes)

Show your work. In order to receive full credit, you must show enough detail to demonstrate a clear under-standing of the concepts involved. You may use a graphing calculator. Where appropriate, you may give numerical answers in exact form or as decimal approximations correct to three decimal places.

1. A particle travels in the xy-plane according to the equations $x(t) = t^3 + 5$ and $y(t) = 4t^2 - 3$ for $t \geq 0$.

   (a) For $t = 5$, find the velocity vector and its magnitude.

   (b) Find the total distance traveled (i.e., the length of the path traced) by the particle during the interval $0 \leq t \leq 5$.

   (c) Find $\dfrac{dy}{dx}$ as a function of t.

   (d) Find $\dfrac{d^2y}{dx^2}$ as a function of t.

2.

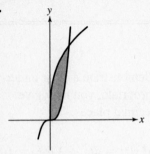

The shaded region is enclosed by the graphs of $y = x^3$ and $y = 4\sqrt[3]{4x}$.

(a) Find the coordinates of the point in the first quadrant where the two curves intersect.

(b) Use an integral with respect to x to find the area of the shaded region.

(c) Write an integral with respect to y that could be used to confirm your answer to part (b).

(d) Without using absolute values, write an integral expression that gives the volume of the solid generated by revolving the shaded region about the line $x = -1$. Do not evaluate.

3.

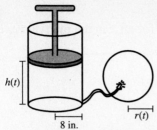

The figure above shows a pump connected by a flexible tube to a spherical balloon. The pump consists of a cylindrical container of radius 8 inches, with a piston that moves up and down according to the equation $h(t) = \dfrac{24}{t+1} + \ln(t+1)$ for $0 \le t \le 100$, where t is measured in seconds and $h(t)$ is measured in inches. As the piston moves up and down, the total volume of air enclosed in the pump and the balloon remains constant, and $r(t) = 0$ at $t = 0$. $\left(\text{The volume of a sphere with radius } r \text{ is } \dfrac{4}{3}\pi r^3.\right)$

(a) Write an expression in terms of $h(t)$ and $r(t)$ for the total volume of the air enclosed in the pump and the balloon. (Do not include the air in the flexible tube.)

(b) Find the rate of change of the volume of the air enclosed in the pump at $t = 3$ sec.

(c) Find the rate of change of the radius of the balloon at $t = 3$ sec.

(d) Find the maximum volume of the balloon and when it occurs.

4. Let f be a function that has derivatives of all orders on the interval $(-1, 1)$.
Assume that $f(0) = 6, f'(0) = 8, f''(0) = 30, f'''(0) = 48$, and $\left|f^{(4)}(x)\right| \le 75$ for all x in the interval $(0, 1)$.

(a) Find the third-order Taylor series about $x = 0$ for $f(x)$.

(b) Use your answer to part (a) to estimate the value of $f(0.2)$.
What is the maximum possible error in making this estimate?

(c) Let $g(x) = xf(x^2)$. Find the Maclaurin series for $g(x)$. (Write as many nonzero terms as possible.)

(d) Let $h(x)$ be a function that has the properties $h(0) = 5$ and $h'(x) = f(x)$.
Find the Maclaurin series for $h(x)$. (Write as many terms as possible.)

5. Consider the family of polar curves defined by $r = 2 + \cos k\theta$, where k is a positive integer.

(a) Show that the area of the region enclosed by the curve does not depend on the value of k. What is the area?

(b) Write an expression in terms of k and θ for the slope $\dfrac{dy}{dx}$ of the curve.

(c) Find the value of $\dfrac{dy}{dx}$ at $\theta = \dfrac{\pi}{4}$, if k is a multiple of 4.

6.

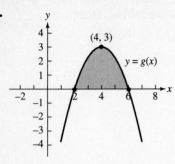

The graph of a differentiable function g is shown. Assume that the area of the shaded region is 8 square units. Let $f(x) = \displaystyle\int_{2}^{x/3 \,+\, 2} g(t)\, dt$.

(a) Find $f(12)$.

(b) Find $f'(6)$.

(c) Write an expression for $f''(x)$ in terms of the function g.

(d) For what values of x is the graph of $y = f(x)$ concave downward? Explain.

(e) Sketch a possible graph for $y = f(x)$.

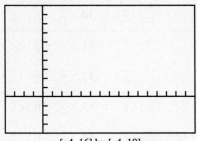

[−4, 16] by [−4, 10]

SAMPLE AB TEST　　　　　## SAMPLE BC TEST

SAMPLE AB TEST		SAMPLE BC TEST	
1. Ⓐ Ⓑ Ⓒ Ⓓ Ⓔ	26. Ⓐ Ⓑ Ⓒ Ⓓ Ⓔ	1. Ⓐ Ⓑ Ⓒ Ⓓ Ⓔ	26. Ⓐ Ⓑ Ⓒ Ⓓ Ⓔ
2. Ⓐ Ⓑ Ⓒ Ⓓ Ⓔ	27. Ⓐ Ⓑ Ⓒ Ⓓ Ⓔ	2. Ⓐ Ⓑ Ⓒ Ⓓ Ⓔ	27. Ⓐ Ⓑ Ⓒ Ⓓ Ⓔ
3. Ⓐ Ⓑ Ⓒ Ⓓ Ⓔ	28. Ⓐ Ⓑ Ⓒ Ⓓ Ⓔ	3. Ⓐ Ⓑ Ⓒ Ⓓ Ⓔ	28. Ⓐ Ⓑ Ⓒ Ⓓ Ⓔ
4. Ⓐ Ⓑ Ⓒ Ⓓ Ⓔ	29. Ⓐ Ⓑ Ⓒ Ⓓ Ⓔ	4. Ⓐ Ⓑ Ⓒ Ⓓ Ⓔ	29. Ⓐ Ⓑ Ⓒ Ⓓ Ⓔ
5. Ⓐ Ⓑ Ⓒ Ⓓ Ⓔ	30. Ⓐ Ⓑ Ⓒ Ⓓ Ⓔ	5. Ⓐ Ⓑ Ⓒ Ⓓ Ⓔ	30. Ⓐ Ⓑ Ⓒ Ⓓ Ⓔ
6. Ⓐ Ⓑ Ⓒ Ⓓ Ⓔ	31. Ⓐ Ⓑ Ⓒ Ⓓ Ⓔ	6. Ⓐ Ⓑ Ⓒ Ⓓ Ⓔ	31. Ⓐ Ⓑ Ⓒ Ⓓ Ⓔ
7. Ⓐ Ⓑ Ⓒ Ⓓ Ⓔ	32. Ⓐ Ⓑ Ⓒ Ⓓ Ⓔ	7. Ⓐ Ⓑ Ⓒ Ⓓ Ⓔ	32. Ⓐ Ⓑ Ⓒ Ⓓ Ⓔ
8. Ⓐ Ⓑ Ⓒ Ⓓ Ⓔ	33. Ⓐ Ⓑ Ⓒ Ⓓ Ⓔ	8. Ⓐ Ⓑ Ⓒ Ⓓ Ⓔ	33. Ⓐ Ⓑ Ⓒ Ⓓ Ⓔ
9. Ⓐ Ⓑ Ⓒ Ⓓ Ⓔ	34. Ⓐ Ⓑ Ⓒ Ⓓ Ⓔ	9. Ⓐ Ⓑ Ⓒ Ⓓ Ⓔ	34. Ⓐ Ⓑ Ⓒ Ⓓ Ⓔ
10. Ⓐ Ⓑ Ⓒ Ⓓ Ⓔ	35. Ⓐ Ⓑ Ⓒ Ⓓ Ⓔ	10. Ⓐ Ⓑ Ⓒ Ⓓ Ⓔ	35. Ⓐ Ⓑ Ⓒ Ⓓ Ⓔ
11. Ⓐ Ⓑ Ⓒ Ⓓ Ⓔ	36. Ⓐ Ⓑ Ⓒ Ⓓ Ⓔ	11. Ⓐ Ⓑ Ⓒ Ⓓ Ⓔ	36. Ⓐ Ⓑ Ⓒ Ⓓ Ⓔ
12. Ⓐ Ⓑ Ⓒ Ⓓ Ⓔ	37. Ⓐ Ⓑ Ⓒ Ⓓ Ⓔ	12. Ⓐ Ⓑ Ⓒ Ⓓ Ⓔ	37. Ⓐ Ⓑ Ⓒ Ⓓ Ⓔ
13. Ⓐ Ⓑ Ⓒ Ⓓ Ⓔ	38. Ⓐ Ⓑ Ⓒ Ⓓ Ⓔ	13. Ⓐ Ⓑ Ⓒ Ⓓ Ⓔ	38. Ⓐ Ⓑ Ⓒ Ⓓ Ⓔ
14. Ⓐ Ⓑ Ⓒ Ⓓ Ⓔ	39. Ⓐ Ⓑ Ⓒ Ⓓ Ⓔ	14. Ⓐ Ⓑ Ⓒ Ⓓ Ⓔ	39. Ⓐ Ⓑ Ⓒ Ⓓ Ⓔ
15. Ⓐ Ⓑ Ⓒ Ⓓ Ⓔ	40. Ⓐ Ⓑ Ⓒ Ⓓ Ⓔ	15. Ⓐ Ⓑ Ⓒ Ⓓ Ⓔ	40. Ⓐ Ⓑ Ⓒ Ⓓ Ⓔ
16. Ⓐ Ⓑ Ⓒ Ⓓ Ⓔ	41. Ⓐ Ⓑ Ⓒ Ⓓ Ⓔ	16. Ⓐ Ⓑ Ⓒ Ⓓ Ⓔ	41. Ⓐ Ⓑ Ⓒ Ⓓ Ⓔ
17. Ⓐ Ⓑ Ⓒ Ⓓ Ⓔ	42. Ⓐ Ⓑ Ⓒ Ⓓ Ⓔ	17. Ⓐ Ⓑ Ⓒ Ⓓ Ⓔ	42. Ⓐ Ⓑ Ⓒ Ⓓ Ⓔ
18. Ⓐ Ⓑ Ⓒ Ⓓ Ⓔ	43. Ⓐ Ⓑ Ⓒ Ⓓ Ⓔ	18. Ⓐ Ⓑ Ⓒ Ⓓ Ⓔ	43. Ⓐ Ⓑ Ⓒ Ⓓ Ⓔ
19. Ⓐ Ⓑ Ⓒ Ⓓ Ⓔ	44. Ⓐ Ⓑ Ⓒ Ⓓ Ⓔ	19. Ⓐ Ⓑ Ⓒ Ⓓ Ⓔ	44. Ⓐ Ⓑ Ⓒ Ⓓ Ⓔ
20. Ⓐ Ⓑ Ⓒ Ⓓ Ⓔ	45. Ⓐ Ⓑ Ⓒ Ⓓ Ⓔ	20. Ⓐ Ⓑ Ⓒ Ⓓ Ⓔ	45. Ⓐ Ⓑ Ⓒ Ⓓ Ⓔ
21. Ⓐ Ⓑ Ⓒ Ⓓ Ⓔ		21. Ⓐ Ⓑ Ⓒ Ⓓ Ⓔ	
22. Ⓐ Ⓑ Ⓒ Ⓓ Ⓔ		22. Ⓐ Ⓑ Ⓒ Ⓓ Ⓔ	
23. Ⓐ Ⓑ Ⓒ Ⓓ Ⓔ		23. Ⓐ Ⓑ Ⓒ Ⓓ Ⓔ	
24. Ⓐ Ⓑ Ⓒ Ⓓ Ⓔ		24. Ⓐ Ⓑ Ⓒ Ⓓ Ⓔ	
25. Ⓐ Ⓑ Ⓒ Ⓓ Ⓔ		25. Ⓐ Ⓑ Ⓒ Ⓓ Ⓔ	

Answers

Concepts Worksheets

Sections 1.2–1.6

1. (a)

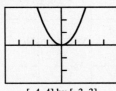

[–4, 4] by [–3, 3]

(b)

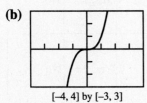

[–4, 4] by [–3, 3]

(c)

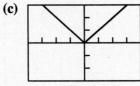

[–4, 4] by [–3, 3]

(d)

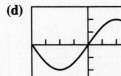

[–π, π] by [–1.5, 1.5]

(e)

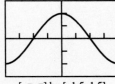

[–π, π] by [–1.5, 1.5]

(f)

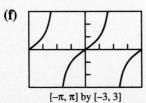

[–π, π] by [–3, 3]

(g)

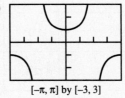

[–π, π] by [–3, 3]

(h)

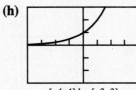

[–4, 4] by [–3, 3]

(i)

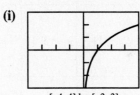

[–4, 4] by [–3, 3]

(j)

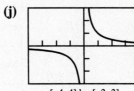

[–4, 4] by [–3, 3]

(k)

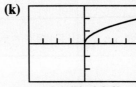

[–4, 4] by [–3, 3]

(l)

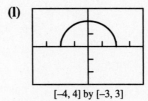

[–4, 4] by [–3, 3]

2.

Function	Domain	Range $y = f(x)$	Zeros (Find x when $f(x) = 0$)	Symmetry with respect to y-axis or origin	Even or Odd Function— $f(-x) = f(x)$ or $f(-x) = -f(x)$	Is the function periodic? If so, state the period.	Is $f(x)$ a one-to-one function? (For each $f(x)$ only one x exists)
(a) $f(x) = x^2$	R	$y \geq 0$	$x = 0$	y-axis	Even	No	No
(b) $f(x) = x^3$	R	R	$x = 0$	Origin	Odd	No	Yes
(c) $f(x) = \lvert x \rvert$	R	$y \geq 0$	$x = 0$	y-axis	Even	No	No
(d) $f(x) = \sin x$	R	$\lvert y \rvert \leq 1$	$x = k\pi,$ $k \in J$	Origin	Odd	Yes, 2π	No
(e) $f(x) = \cos x$	R	$\lvert y \rvert \leq 1$	$x = (2k+1)\dfrac{\pi}{2},$ $k \in J$	y-axis	Even	Yes, 2π	No
(f) $f(x) = \tan x$	$x \in R,$ $x \neq (2k+1)\dfrac{\pi}{2},$ $k \in J$	R	$x = k\pi,$ $k \in J$	Origin	Odd	Yes, π	No
(g) $f(x) = \sec x$	$x \in R,$ $x \neq (2k+1)\dfrac{\pi}{2},$ $k \in J$	$\lvert y \rvert \geq 1$	None	y-axis	Even	Yes, 2π	No
(h) $f(x) = 2^x$	R	$y > 0$	None	Neither	Neither	No	Yes
(i) $f(x) = \log_2 x$	$x > 0$	R	$x = 1$	Neither	Neither	No	Yes
(j) $f(x) = \dfrac{1}{x}$	$x \in R,$ $x \neq 0$	$y \in R,$ $y \neq 0$	None	Origin	Odd	No	Yes
(k) $f(x) = \sqrt{x}$	$x \geq 0$	$y \geq 0$	$x = 0$	Neither	Neither	No	Yes
(l) $f(x) = \sqrt{a^2 - x^2}$	$\lvert x \rvert \leq a$	$0 \leq y \leq a$	$x = \pm a$	y-axis	Even	No	No

3. Yes. Even functions have *y*-axis symmetry, while odd functions are symmetric about the origin.

4. (a) 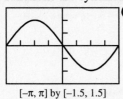   **(b)**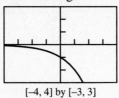

$[-\pi, \pi]$ by $[-1.5, 1.5]$ $[-4, 4]$ by $[-3, 3]$

(c)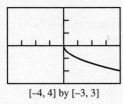

$[-4, 4]$ by $[-3, 3]$

5. (a) 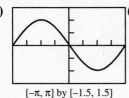   **(b)**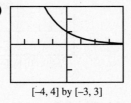

$[-\pi, \pi]$ by $[-1.5, 1.5]$ $[-4, 4]$ by $[-3, 3]$

(c)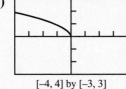

$[-4, 4]$ by $[-3, 3]$

Section 1.4

1. 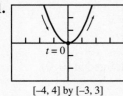   **2.**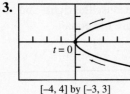

$[-4, 4]$ by $[-3, 3]$ $[-4, 4]$ by $[-3, 3]$

3. 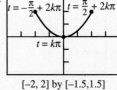   **4.**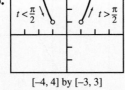

$[-4, 4]$ by $[-3, 3]$ $[-4, 4]$ by $[-3, 3]$

5. 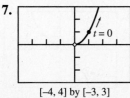   **6.**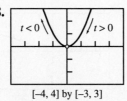

$[-2, 2]$ by $[-1.5, 1.5]$ $[-4, 4]$ by $[-3, 3]$

7.   **8.**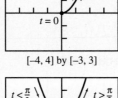

$[-4, 4]$ by $[-3, 3]$ $[-4, 4]$ by $[-3, 3]$

9. $x = g(t)$, $y = f(t)$; 3
10. $x = e^{2t}$, $y = e^{t}$

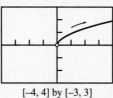

$[-4, 4]$ by $[-3, 3]$

11. (a) One possible answer:
$x = t^2$, $y = -t$
(b) One possible answer:
$x = t^2$, $y = |t|$

Sections 2.2–2.3

1. Left end behavior model
2. Both
3. Neither
4. Right end behavior model
5. (a) Continuous at $x = c$
   (b) Discontinuous at $x = c$; removable discontinuity
   (c) Discontinuous at $x = c$; removable discontinuity
   (d) Discontinuous at $x = c$; jump discontinuity
   (e) Discontinuous at $x = c$; infinite discontinuity
   (f) Discontinuous at $x = c$; infinite discontinuity
6. Possible answers:
   (a) $f(x) = \dfrac{1}{x}$
   (b) $f(x) = \dfrac{1}{x^2 - 4}$
   (c) $f(x) = \tan x$
7. Possible answers:
   (a) $f(x) = 3x^2 - 5$
   (b) $f(x) = \begin{cases} 0, & \text{if } x \text{ is rational} \\ 1, & \text{if } x \text{ is irrational} \end{cases}$

Sections 3.1–3.3

1. (a) $\dfrac{2}{3}$ **(b)** $2\pi + 5$

   (c) $15 - 8\pi$ **(d)** $\dfrac{37}{6}$

   (e) -1 **(f)** $\dfrac{\sqrt{2}}{24}$

   (g) $-\dfrac{5}{16}$ **(h)** $-\dfrac{4\sqrt{17}}{51}$

2. (a)

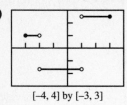

[−4, 4] by [−3, 3]

(b) $x = -2, x = 1$

3. (a) None   **(b)** $x = 0$

(c) $x = 0$ **(d)** $x = 0$

(e) $x \leq 0, x = 1$ **(f)** $x = 0$

4. Corner points, cusp points, very sharply changing points, as well as points at which the function is discontinuous or the tangent line is vertical.

Section 3.4

1. (a) $2 < t < 4$

(b) $4 < t < 6$

(c) $0 \leq t < 2, 6 < t \leq 7$

(d) Velocity(in./sec)

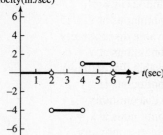

Speed(in./sec)

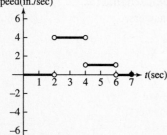

(e) $2 < t < 4$

2. (a) At $t = 1$ sec and at $t \approx 4.25$ sec

(b) $5 < t \leq 6$ **(c)** $t = 3$ sec

(d) $a(\text{m/sec}^2)$

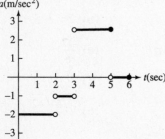

3. (a) 12 cm   **(b)** 2 cm/sec

(c) $\text{v}(t) = t^2 - 6t + 8; a(t) = 2t - 6$

(d) $2 < t < 4$

4. (a) $s(\text{ft})$

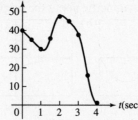

(b) −10 ft/sec; −10 ft/sec; −29 ft/sec

(c) $t \approx 1$ sec, $t \approx 2$ sec

(d) $t \approx 3.5$ sec

5. (a) $t = 3, x = 36; t = 7, x = 4$

(b)

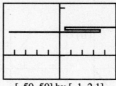

[−50, 50] by [−1, 2.1]

Section 3.7

1. $\dfrac{dy}{dx} = \dfrac{y^2 - 5x^4 - 4x^3 y}{x^4 - 2xy - 3y^2}$

2. (a) -1

(b) -1

(c) 4

3.

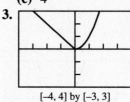

[−4, 4] by [−3, 3]

4. No; The expression is undefined at $(0, 0)$.

5. 0

6. -1

7. No; $f'(0)$ does not exist because the right- and left-hand derivatives at $x = 0$ are not equal.

8. 2; 3

9. $f(x) = 0$

Section 3.8

1.

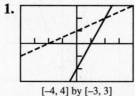

[−4, 4] by [−3, 3]

2.

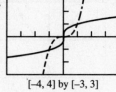

[−4, 4] by [−3, 3]

3.

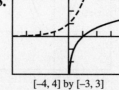

[−4, 4] by [−3, 3]

4.

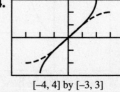

[−4, 4] by [−3, 3]

5. c, d, e, f

6. e, f

7. Each is the inverse function of the other.

8. $g'(x) = \dfrac{1}{f'(g(x))}$

9.

x	$g(x)$	$g'(x)$
-3	1	$\dfrac{1}{4}$
1	2	$\dfrac{1}{5}$
2	3	$\dfrac{1}{6}$

10. $y = 4x - 7$

11. $y = \dfrac{1}{5}x + \dfrac{9}{5}$

12. $y = -6x + 15$

Section 3.9

1. $\displaystyle\lim_{h \to 0} \frac{3^{x+h} - 3^x}{h}, \lim_{h \to 0} \frac{3^x \cdot 3^h - 3^x}{h}, \lim_{h \to 0} \frac{3^x(3^h - 1)}{h}$

2.

h	1	-1	0.1	-0.1	0.01	-0.01	0.001	-0.001	0.0001	-0.0001
$\dfrac{2^h-1}{h}$	1	0.50	0.718	0.670	0.696	0.691	0.6934	0.6929	0.6932	0.6931
$\dfrac{3^h-1}{h}$	2	0.667	1.161	1.040	1.105	1.093	1.099	1.098	1.0987	1.0986

3. 0.693; 1.099

4. $(e^{\ln 2})^x = e^{x \ln 2}$; $e^{x \ln 2} (\ln 2) = 2^x(\ln 2)$; $\ln 2$

5. $(e^{\ln 3})^x = e^{x \ln 3}$; $e^{x \ln 3} (\ln 3) = 3^x(\ln 3)$; $\ln 3$

6. $(e^{\ln x})^x = e^{x \ln x}$;

$$e^{x \ln x}\left(x \cdot \frac{1}{x} + \ln x\right) = x^x(1 + \ln x)$$

Section 4.1

1. (a) $x = a, c, g, k$

(b) $x = h$

(c) $x = b, d, f, h \le x \le i, x = j, k, m$

(d) $[b, f], [j, k], [m, \infty)$

(e) $(-\infty, b], [f, h), [i, j], [k, m]$

(f) $x = f, h \le x \le i, x = k$

(g) One possible answer: $x = f$

(Answer may depend on assumptions made regarding the end behavior of the function.)

(h) $x = b, h \le x \le i, x = j, x = m$

(i) None

(j) $(d, e), (l, n)$

(k) $(-\infty, b), (b, d), (e, h), (j, l), (n, \infty)$

(l) $x = d, e, l, n$

2. (a) $y = 0$ (and possibly $y = p$ for some positive constant p)

(b) $x = h$

3. $x = b, h, i, j$

4. $x = b, d, e, h \le x \le j, x = l, n$

5.

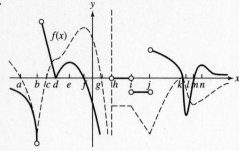

Section 4.2

1. (a)

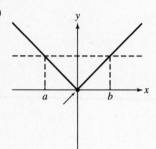

(b)

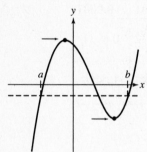

(c)

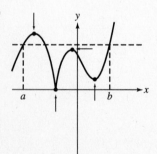

(d) The variation of Rolle's Theorem does not apply because $f(a) \ne f(b)$.

2. (a)

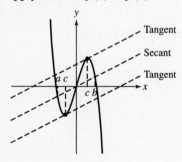

(b)

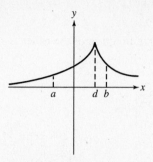

The Mean Value Theorem does not apply, because the function is not differentiable at $x = d$.

(c)

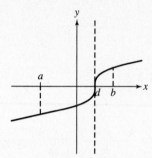

It appears that the graph is not differentiable at $x = d$. The Mean Value Theorem does not apply.

(d) Every point between a and b would be an appropriate c in the Mean Value Theorem, since the tangent line coincides with the secant line for every c.

(e) The Mean Value Theorem does not apply, because the function is not differentiable at $x = 0$.

3. (a) Applying the Mean Value Theorem with $a = 1$ and $b = 3$, there is at least one value of c in $(1, 3)$ such that

$$f'(c) = \frac{f(3) - f(1)}{3 - 1} = \frac{7 - 5}{3 - 1} = 1.$$

(b) Since $f'(x)$ is continuous and differentiable, we may apply the Mean Value Theorem to $f'(x)$ with $a = 1$ and $b = 3$. There is at least one value of c in $(1, 3)$ such that

$$f''(c) = \frac{f'(3) - f'(1)}{3 - 1} = \frac{-1 - 2}{3 - 1} = -\frac{3}{2}.$$

Section 4.3

1.

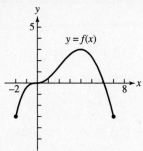

2. One possible answer:

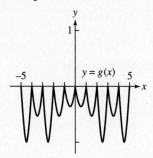

3.

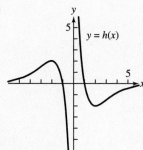

4. (a) Origin; $-f(x)$ **(b)** 0
     (c) 0   **(d)** $\pm 5a$
     (e) $\pm 2a, 0$ **(f)** $(2a, 6a)$

Section 5.2

1. $\int_0^1 x^2\, dx$ **2.** $\int_0^1 (x + x^2)\, dx$

3. $\int_0^1 \sqrt{1 + 2x}\, dx$ **4.** $\int_1^2 \frac{1}{2x}\, dx$ or $\frac{1}{2}\int_0^1 \frac{dx}{1 + x}$

5. $\int_0^2 \frac{1}{1 + 2x}\, dx$ **6.** $\int_0^2 \frac{1}{1 + 2x}\, dx$

7. $\frac{1}{2}\int_0^4 \frac{1}{1 + x}\, dx$ **8.** $\frac{1}{2}\int_1^5 \frac{1}{x}\, dx$

9. Yes, because they can all be represented by the same limit of Riemann sums.

Sections 5.3–5.4

1.

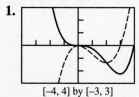

[–4, 4] by [–3, 3]

2.

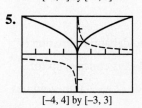

[–4, 4] by [–3, 3]

3.

[–4, 4] by [–3, 3]

4.

[–4, 4] by [–3, 3]

5.

[–4, 4] by [–3, 3]

6. c   **7.** d
8. a   **9.** b
10. (a) 0   **(b)** Increasing
      (c) $0 < x < 1$ **(d)** None
      (e)

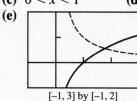

[–1, 3] by [–1, 2]

11. (a) 0   **(b)** 0
      (c) 1   **(d)** $\frac{1}{2}$
      (e) $\frac{3}{2}$
      (f) $0 < x < \frac{1}{2}, \frac{3}{2} < x < 2$
      (g) $\frac{1}{2} < x < \frac{3}{2}$
      (h)

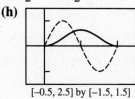

[–0.5, 2.5] by [–1.5, 1.5]

12. (a) 0   **(b)** $2b$
    (c) $2b$

13.

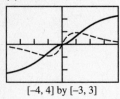

[–4, 4] by [–3, 3]

Section 5.4

1. $\dfrac{1}{1+x^2}$ **2.** $2\sqrt{4x^2+1}$

3. 0   **4.** $\dfrac{\sin x}{2\sqrt{x}}$

5. $-\dfrac{2}{x}$ **6.** $\sqrt{15}$

7. $\sqrt{6}$ **8.** $\dfrac{1}{2}$

Section 5.5

1. $\displaystyle\int_0^2 x^3\,dx = 4$. The trapezoidal approximation is greater since $y = x^3$ is always concave up for $0 \le x \le 2$ and the top side of each trapezoid lies above the curve.

2. $\displaystyle\int_2^{20} \dfrac{x}{4}\,dx = \int_1^{10} x\,dx = \dfrac{99}{2}$. The trapezoidal approximation would equal the integral answer since the function being integrated represents a straight line which the trapezoids would exactly fit.

3. (a) $\displaystyle\int_0^4 \sqrt{x}\,dx = \dfrac{16}{3}$

    (b) $\dfrac{1}{4}\Bigg[0 + 2\left(\dfrac{\sqrt{2}}{2}\right) + 2(1) + 2\left(\dfrac{\sqrt{6}}{2}\right) + 2(\sqrt{2})$

         $+ 2\left(\dfrac{\sqrt{10}}{2}\right) + 2(\sqrt{3}) + 2\left(\dfrac{\sqrt{14}}{2}\right) + 2\Bigg]$

    (c) Note that $f(x) = \sqrt{x}$ is concave down. Since the Trapezoidal Rule approximation is based on straight segments which lie below the graph of $y = f(x)$ and the Simpson's Rule approximation is based on curves which nearly match the graph of $y = f(x)$, expect the Simpson's Rule approximation to be larger. To confirm, observe that $S \approx 5.3046$ and $T \approx 5.2650$.

4. Let $\Delta x = \dfrac{b-a}{n}$. The inscribed rectangular area approximation is

$$I = [f(x_0) + f(x_1) + f(x_2) + \cdots + f(x_{n-1})]\Delta x,$$

and the circumscribed retangular area approximation is

$$C = [f(x_1) + f(x_2) + f(x_3) + \cdots + f(x_n)]\Delta x.$$

Therefore,

$$\dfrac{I+C}{2} = \dfrac{1}{2}\Big[f(x_0) + 2f(x_1) + 2f(x_2) + \cdots$$
$$+ 2f(x_{n-1}) + f(x_n)\Big]\Delta x$$
$$= \dfrac{b-a}{2n}\Big[f(x_0) + 2f(x_1) + 2f(x_2) + \cdots$$
$$+ 2f(x_{n-1}) + f(x_n)\Big].$$

Sections 6.1–6.2

1.

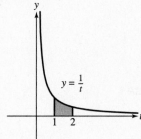

$y = \dfrac{1}{t}$

2.

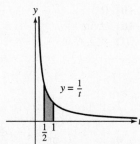

$y = \dfrac{1}{t}$

3. (a) $\displaystyle\int_1^x \dfrac{1}{t}\,dt = \ln x$

    (b) $\displaystyle\int_1^1 \dfrac{1}{t}\,dt = 0$

    (c) $\displaystyle\int_x^1 \dfrac{1}{t}\,dt = -\ln x$

4. (a)

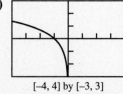

[–4, 4] by [–3, 3]

(b)

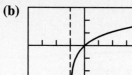

[–4, 4] by [–3, 3]

(c)

[–4, 4] by [–3, 3]

5. (a)

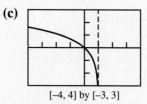

$y = \dfrac{1}{t}$

[–4, 4] by [–3, 3]

(b)

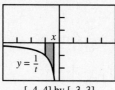

$y = \dfrac{1}{1+t}$

[–4, 4] by [–3, 3]

(c)

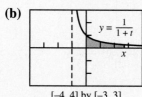

$y = \dfrac{1}{1-t}$

[–4, 4] by [–3, 3]

6. (a) $\ln |x|$ **(b)** $\ln (1 + x)$
(c) $-\ln (1 - x)$

7. If $t = au$, then $dt = a\,du$. Therefore, when $t = a$,

$u = 1$ and when $t = ax$, $u = x$.

$$\int_a^{ax} \frac{1}{t}\,dt = \int_1^x \frac{1}{au} \cdot a\,du = \int_1^x \frac{du}{u}$$

$$\int_a^{ax} \frac{1}{t}\,dt = \ln t \Big|_a^{ax} = \ln (ax) - \ln (a)$$

$$\int_1^x \frac{du}{u} = \ln u \Big|_1^x = \ln x - \ln 1 = \ln x$$

Therefore, $\ln (ax) - \ln (a) = \ln x$, so

$\ln (ax) = \ln x + \ln (a)$.

Sections 7.1–7.5

1. (a) $\displaystyle\int_0^{60} R(t)\,dt$ **(b)** 842.5 cm

2. (a) ≈ 4.6; 4.6 inches of rain fell during the
24 hours beginning at midnight.
(b) ≈ 1.2; 1.2 inches of rain fell between 4 A.M.
and noon.
(c) ≈ 2.5; 2.5 inches of rain fell between 8 A.M.
and 8 P.M.

3. $2,500,000   **4.** 3200 ft-lb

Section 7.2

1. $\displaystyle\int_a^b f(x)\,dx$

2. $\displaystyle\int_a^0 [g(x) - f(x)]\,dx + \int_0^b [f(x) - g(x)]\,dx$

3. $-\displaystyle\int_a^b f(x)\,dx$ or $\displaystyle\int_b^a f(x)\,dx$

4. $-\displaystyle\int_a^c f(x)\,dx + \int_c^b f(x)\,dx$

5. $\displaystyle\int_a^b [f(x) - g(x)]\,dx$

6. $\displaystyle\int_a^b [f(x) - g(x)]\,dx$

7. $\displaystyle\int_a^c [g(x) - f(x)]\,dx + \int_c^b [f(x) - g(x)]\,dx$

8. $\displaystyle\int_c^d [g(y) - f(y)]\,dy$

9. $2\displaystyle\int_0^a f(y)\,dy$ or $\displaystyle\int_{-a}^a f(y)\,dy$

10. $\dfrac{32}{3}$

Section 7.3

1. (a)

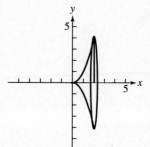

(b)

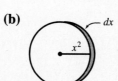

(c) πx^4 **(d)** $\pi x^4\,dx$

(e) $\pi \displaystyle\int_0^2 x^4\,dx$ **(f)** $\dfrac{32\pi}{5}$

2. (a)

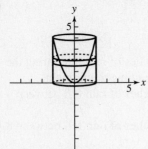

(b)

(c) $4\pi - \pi y$ **(d)** $\pi(4 - y)\,dy$

(e) $\pi \int_0^4 (4 - y)\,dy$ **(f)** 8π

3. (a)

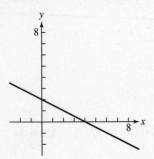

(b)

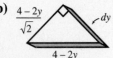

(c) $\dfrac{1}{2}\left(\dfrac{4-2y}{\sqrt{2}}\right)^2 = (2-y)^2$

(d) $(2-y)^2\,dy$

(e) $\displaystyle\int_0^2 (2-y)^2\,dy$

(f) $\dfrac{8}{3}$

4. (a) $f(x)$

(b) $2\pi x$

(c) $2\pi x f(x)$

(d) $2\pi x f(x)\,dx$

(e) $2\pi \displaystyle\int_a^b x f(x)\,dx$

Sections 9.1–9.5

1. (a) $-\dfrac{1}{2} < x \le \dfrac{1}{2}$

(b) $f\left(\dfrac{1}{4}\right) = \dfrac{1}{2} - \dfrac{1}{8} + \dfrac{1}{24} - \cdots$
$$+ \dfrac{(-1)^{n+1}}{n}\left(\dfrac{1}{2}\right)^n + \cdots$$

(c) $\ln\left(\dfrac{3}{2}\right)$

(d) $f'(x) = 2 - 4x + 8x^2 - \cdots$
$$+ (-1)^{n+1}(2)(2x)^{n-1} + \cdots\,;$$
$$f'\left(\dfrac{1}{4}\right) = \dfrac{4}{3}$$

2. (a) $7 - 3(x-3) + 6(x-3)^2$

(b) $8.44;\ 0.162$

(c) $-2 + 7(x-3) - \dfrac{3}{2}(x-3)^2 + 2(x-3)^3$

(d) $7x^2 - 3x^3 + 6x^4$

3. (a) $f'(x) = 5 - 3x - \dfrac{5}{2!}x^2 + \dfrac{3}{3!}x^3 + \dfrac{5}{4!}x^4$
$$- \dfrac{3}{5!}x^5 - \dfrac{5}{6!}x^6 + \cdots$$
$$+ (-1)^n\left[\dfrac{3}{(2n-1)!}x^{2n-1}\right.$$
$$+ \left.\dfrac{5}{(2n)!}x^{2n}\right] + \cdots$$

$$f''(x) = -3 - 5x + \dfrac{3}{2!}x^2 + \dfrac{5}{3!}x^3 - \dfrac{3}{4!}x^4$$
$$- \dfrac{5}{5!}x^5 + \cdots$$
$$+ (-1)^n\left[\dfrac{3}{(2n-2)!}x^{2n-2}\right.$$
$$+ \left.\dfrac{5}{(2n-1)!}x^{2n-1}\right] + \cdots$$

Note that, if n is replaced by $n + 2$ in the general term for $f''(x)$, we obtain the opposite of the general term for $f(x)$. This means that $f''(x) = -f(x)$, so $y = f(x)$ solves $y'' + y = 0$.

(b) All real numbers

(c) $f(x) = 3\cos x + 5\sin x$

Section 10.3

1. (a) $(-\sqrt{2}, 2), (\sqrt{2}, 2)$

(b) $(0, 0)$

(c) $(0, 0), \left(\dfrac{\sqrt{6}}{2}, \dfrac{3}{2}\right), \left(-\dfrac{\sqrt{6}}{2}, \dfrac{3}{2}\right)$

(d)

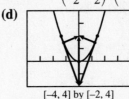

$[-4, 4]$ by $[-2, 4]$

2. (a) $v\left(\dfrac{\pi}{6}\right) = r'\left(\dfrac{\pi}{6}\right) = \left(\dfrac{-\sqrt{3}}{2}\right)\mathbf{i} + \left(-\dfrac{3}{2}\right)\mathbf{j}$

$a\left(\dfrac{\pi}{6}\right) = r''\left(\dfrac{\pi}{6}\right) = \dfrac{1}{2}\mathbf{i} + \left(\dfrac{-3\sqrt{3}}{2}\right)\mathbf{j}$

(b) $r\left(\dfrac{\pi}{6}\right) = \dfrac{3}{2}\mathbf{i} + \dfrac{3\sqrt{3}}{2}\mathbf{j}$

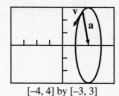

[−4, 4] by [−3, 3]

(c) minimum $t = 0,\ \pi,\ 2\pi$

maximum $t = \dfrac{\pi}{2},\ \dfrac{3}{2}\pi$

3. (a) $(t^2)\mathbf{i} + (t^3 - 1)\mathbf{j}$

(b)

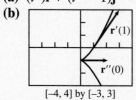

[−4, 4] by [−3, 3]

(c) $r'(1) = 2\mathbf{i} + 3\mathbf{j}$

(d) $r''(t) = 2\mathbf{i} + 6t\mathbf{j}$, $r''(0) = 2\mathbf{i} + 0\mathbf{j}$

(e) There exist none since the **i** component of the vector is always nonzero.

4. (a) $r(t) = (C_1 e^t)\mathbf{i} + (C_2 e^t)\mathbf{j}$ where C_1, C_2 are arbitrary constants.

(b) $r(t) = (C_1 e^{-t})\mathbf{i} + (C_2 e^{-t})\mathbf{j}$ where C_1, C_2 are arbitrary constants.

Section 10.5

1. (a)

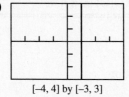

[−4, 4] by [−3, 3]

(b)

[−4, 4] by [−3, 3]

(c)

[−4, 4] by [−3, 3]

2. (a)

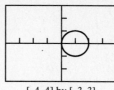

[−4, 4] by [−3, 3]

(b)

[−4, 4] by [−3, 3]

(c)

[−4, 4] by [−3, 3]

3. (a)

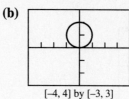

[−4, 4] by [−3, 3]

(b)

[−4, 4] by [−3, 3]

4.

[−4, 4] by [−3, 3]

5. (a)

[−4, 4] by [−3, 3]

(b)

[−4, 4] by [−3, 3]

(c)

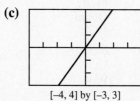

[−4, 4] by [−3, 3]

6. (a)

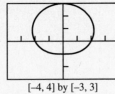

[−4, 4] by [−3, 3]

$r = 2 + \sin \theta$

(b)

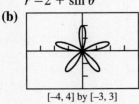

[−4, 4] by [−3, 3]

$r = 2 \sin 5\theta$

Section 10.6

1. (a) $x = (1 + \cos \theta) \cos \theta$, $y = (1 + \cos \theta) \sin \theta$

(b) $\dfrac{dx}{d\theta} = -\sin \theta - 2 \sin \theta \cos \theta$

$= -\sin \theta - \sin 2\theta;$

$\dfrac{dy}{d\theta} = \cos \theta + \cos^2 \theta - \sin^2 \theta$

$= \cos \theta + \cos 2\theta$

(c) $\dfrac{\cos \theta + \cos 2\theta}{-\sin \theta - \sin 2\theta}$

(d) $y = x + 1$

(e) $y = 1 - x$

2. (a) $x = -\cos^2 \theta$, $y = -\cos \theta \sin \theta$

(b) $\dfrac{dx}{d\theta} = 2 \sin \theta \cos \theta = \sin 2\theta,$

$\dfrac{dy}{d\theta} = -\cos^2 \theta + \sin^2 \theta = -\cos 2\theta$

(c) $\dfrac{-\cos 2\theta}{\sin 2\theta} = -\cot 2\theta$

(d) $\dfrac{\pi}{4}, \dfrac{3\pi}{4}$

(e) $0, \dfrac{\pi}{2}, \pi$

3. To find point of intersection: $2 \cos \theta = 2 \sin \theta$

$\theta = \dfrac{\pi}{4}$ or at the pole

for $r = 2 \cos \theta$,

$\dfrac{dy}{dx} = \dfrac{2 \cos^2 \theta - 2 \sin^2 \theta}{-4 \sin \theta \cos \theta} = \dfrac{2 \cos 2\theta}{-2 \sin 2\theta} = -\cot 2\theta$

$\dfrac{dy}{dx} = 0$ at $\theta = \dfrac{\pi}{4}$

for $r = 2 \sin \theta$,

$\dfrac{dy}{dx} = \dfrac{4 \sin \theta \cos \theta}{2 \cos 2\theta} = \tan 2\theta$

$\dfrac{dy}{dx}$ is undefined (vertical slope) at $\theta = \dfrac{\pi}{4}$.

Therefore, the slopes of the tangents at $\theta = \dfrac{\pi}{4}$

indicate the lines are perpendicular.

At the pole:

$r = 2 \cos \theta$ and $r = 2 \sin \theta$ intersect for different values at θ, namely $\theta = \dfrac{\pi}{2}$ and $\theta = 0$, respectively. Slope of the tangent to $r = 2 \cos \theta$ at $\theta = \dfrac{\pi}{2}$ is undefined. Slope of the tangent to $r = 2 \sin \theta$ at $\theta = 0$ is 0. Therefore, the slopes indicate the tangent are perpendicular at the pole.

4. (a) $\theta = \dfrac{\pi}{2}, \dfrac{3\pi}{2}, \sin^{-1} \dfrac{3}{5}, \pi - \sin^{-1} \dfrac{3}{5}$

(b)

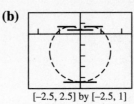

[−2.5, 2.5] by [−2.5, 1]

5.

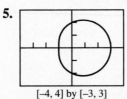

[−4, 4] by [−3, 3]

Point closest to the pole is at $(1, \pi)$, and line tangent to $r = 2 + \cos \theta$ at this point is vertical. For the "dimpling effect" we are interested in any other vertical tangents symmetrically situated on the curve about $\theta = \pi$. The only other vertical tangent occurs when $\theta = 0$. Therefore, there is no dimple around $\theta = \pi$.

6. $1 \le a < 2$

Group Activity Explorations

Chapter 1 Review

Here is one possible solution:

A: 4	B: 6
C: 10	D: 18
E: 1	F: $y = 4x + 1$
G: $-\dfrac{1}{4}$	H: $y = -\dfrac{1}{4}x + 18$
I: 1	J: $\dfrac{1}{4}$
K: −1	
L: Denmark	M: 8
N: 1	O: tan
P: π	Q: 0
R: 0	S: 1
T: 162	U: 9
V: SINE	W: U
X: 1	

Special message: You won!

Section 2.3

A

1. When x takes on only irrational values, $f(x) = 0$ and $\lim_{x \to 0} 0 = 0$.

2. When x takes on only rational values, $f(x) = x$ and $\lim_{x \to 0} x = 0$.

3. $\lim_{x \to a} 0 = 0$ and $\lim_{x \to a} a = a$.

4. Since $\lim_{x \to a} 0 = \lim_{x \to a} a$ only when $a = 0$, $f(x)$ is continuous only at $x = 0$.

B

1. When x is any integer multiple of π, $\sin x = 0$.

2. $f(x) = \begin{cases} \sin \pi x, & \text{if } x \text{ is rational} \\ 0, & \text{if } x \text{ is irrational} \end{cases}$

3. $f(x) = \text{int } x$ (the step function).

C

1. $f(x) = \begin{cases} x^2 - 4, & \text{if } x \text{ is rational} \\ 0, & \text{if } x \text{ is irrational} \end{cases}$

2. $f(x) = \begin{cases} x^3 - x, & \text{if } x \text{ is rational} \\ 0, & \text{if } x \text{ is irrational} \end{cases}$

3. $f(x) = \begin{cases} \sin \dfrac{\pi x}{2}, & \text{if } x \text{ is rational} \\ 0, & \text{if } x \text{ is irrational} \end{cases}$

D $f(x)$ is continuous when $x = \pm\dfrac{1}{n}$, where n is a positive integer.

Section 3.1

1. $f'(x) = \lim_{h \to 0} \dfrac{f(x + h) - f(x)}{h}$

$= \lim_{h \to 0} \dfrac{f(x) + f(h) + 2xh - f(x)}{h}$

$= \lim_{h \to 0} \dfrac{f(h) + 2xh}{h} = \lim_{h \to 0} \dfrac{f(h)}{h} + \dfrac{2xh}{h} = 10 + 2x$

2. One possible answer: $f(x) = x^2 + 10x$

3. One possible answer: $f(x) = x^2 + 10x + 1$

4. $f(x) = x^2 + 10x + C$; C is any real number.

5. $f(0 + h) = f(0) + f(h) + 2 \cdot 0 \cdot h$
$f(h) = f(0) + f(h) + 0$
$0 = f(0) + 0$
$f(0) = 0$

6. $f(x) = x^2 + 10x$

7. $f(x + h) = (x + h)^2 + 10(x + h)$
$= x^2 + 2xh + h^2 + 10x + 10h$
$= x^2 + 10x + h^2 + 10h + 2xh$
$= f(x) + f(h) + 2xh$

8. $f(x) = 2x^2 + 10x$ **9.** $f(x) = x^2 + 20x$

10. $f(x) = \dfrac{A}{2}x^2 + Bx$

Section 4.4

1.

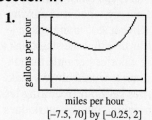

miles per hour
[–7.5, 70] by [–0.25, 2]

2. This makes sense because a car consumes more fuel when traveling very slow or very fast compared to traveling at a moderate speed.

3. The critical point is approximately (36.84, 0.95). The consumption rate C (in gallons/hour) is minimized.

4. $\dfrac{y}{x} = \dfrac{C(v) \text{ gallons/hour}}{v \text{ miles/hour}} = \dfrac{C(v)}{v}$ gallons/mile

5. One possible answer:

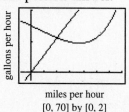

miles per hour
[0, 70] by [0, 2]

The slope of this line represents the number of *gallons per mile* at the chosen speed.

6. Gallons per mile is not minimized at the critical point because the slope of the line through a point on the graph and the origin is not minimized at the critical point.

7. When the slope of the line through a point on the graph and the origin is minimized, fuel consumption will be minimized at that point. This occurs when the line is tangent to the graph.

8.
$$C'(v) = \frac{C(v)}{v}$$

$$4v^3 \times 10^{-7} - 0.02 = v^3 \times 10^{-7} - 0.02 + \frac{1.5}{v}$$

$$4v^3 \times 10^{-7} = v^3 \times 10^{-7} + \frac{1.5}{v}$$

$$3v^3 \times 10^{-7} = \frac{1.5}{v}$$

$$v^4 = \frac{1.5}{3 \times 10^{-7}}$$

$$v = \left(\frac{1.5}{3 \times 10^{-7}}\right)^{1/4} \approx 47.287$$

9. One possible answer: A calculator cannot determine the velocity that optimizes fuel consumption given this equation because the minimum value of the graph does not correspond to the optimum velocity.

10. One possible answer: When a shark starts at zero velocity, it must expend extra energy to overcome inertia. Once it is moving it requires less energy to stay moving, but it must expend increasingly more energy against the water resistance as it swims faster.

11. One possible answer: The graph shows us that a shark is expending less energy when it is moving slowly than when it is staying still in the water.

12. One possible answer: It is true that the shark has to swim faster to minimize calories per mile than to minimize calories per hour. It would always make sense to minimize calories per hour (requiring less feeding) if that were an option, but the shark does not have that luxury. It must cover great distances to "graze" for food. That is why it depends on the circumstances. When it is hunting, it should minimize calories per mile; when it is resting, it should minimze calories per hour.

Section 5.4

1. $P = (h, r)$

2.

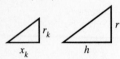

3. $V = \pi(\text{radius})^2(\text{height}) = \pi\left(\dfrac{r}{h}x_k\right)^2 \Delta x$

4. $\displaystyle\lim_{n\to\infty}\sum_{k=1}^{n} \dfrac{\pi r^2}{h^2}x_k^2\, \Delta x = \int_0^h \dfrac{\pi r^2}{h^2}x^2\, dx$

5. Since we are evaluating the integral with respect to x, $\dfrac{\pi r^2}{h^2}$ is a constant. It is always safe to move a constant factor of the integrand outside of the integral.

6. $\dfrac{\pi r^2}{h^2}\displaystyle\int_0^h x^2\, dx = \dfrac{\pi r^2}{h^2}\cdot\dfrac{h^3}{3} = \dfrac{1}{3}\pi r^2 h$

7. radius $= r$; height $= h$

8. Since we are adding the same discs, the Riemann sum is unchanged:
$\displaystyle\lim_{n\to\infty}\sum_{k=1}^{n}\dfrac{\pi r^2}{h^2}x_k^2\, \Delta x = \int_0^h \dfrac{\pi r^2}{h^2}x^2\, dx$

9. $V = \dfrac{1}{3}\pi r^2 h$

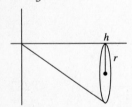

Section 6.1

I.

1. For $\dfrac{dy}{dx} = x + y$, the slope should be zero where $y = -x$. For $\dfrac{dy}{dx} = x - y$, the slope should be zero where $y = x$.

2. Graph A is the slope field of $\dfrac{dy}{dx} = x + y$, and graph B is the slope field of $\dfrac{dy}{dx} = x - y$.

3. As you move to the right, x increases, so the values of $x + y$ and $x - y$ are both increasing.

II.

1. The slope is always positive because 1.1^{x^2} and 1.1^{y^2} are always positive.

2. Graph A shows slopes that depend on x but not on y, and graph B shows slopes that depend on y but not on x.

3. Graph A is the slope field of $\dfrac{dy}{dx} = 1.1^{x^2}$, and graph B is the slope field of $\dfrac{dy}{dx} = 1.1^{y^2}$.

4. For either differential equation, the solution that passes through $(0, 0)$ would be an odd function, while all other solutions would be neither odd nor even.

III.

1. Because both equations depend on y but not on x.

2. Graph A is the slope field of $\dfrac{dy}{dx} = \sin(y^3)$, and graph B is the slope field of $\dfrac{dy}{dx} = \sin(y^2)$. You can tell because $\sin(y^2)$ is an even function of y, meaning that the slope shown at any point (x, y) is the same as the slope shown at $(x, -y)$. Since $\sin(y^3)$ is an odd function of y, the slope shown at any point (x, y) is the opposite of the slope shown at $(x, -y)$.

3. No. Both $\cos(y^2)$ and $\cos(y^3)$ are even functions of y.

IV.

1. Graph A is the slope field of $\dfrac{dy}{dx} = \cos(xy)$, and graph B is the slope field of $\dfrac{dy}{dx} = \sin(xy)$.

2. Since $\sin(0) = 0$, the slopes representing $\dfrac{dy}{dx} = \sin(xy)$ should be zero along the axes, and since $\cos(0) = 1$, the slopes representing $\dfrac{dy}{dx} = \cos(xy)$ should be 1 along the axes.

3. Since the sine function is odd, changing the sign of x or y should change the sign of the slope, as shown in graph B. Since the cosine function is even, the slope shown at any point should be the same as the slope at any corresponding point on the other side of either axis, as shown in graph A.

Section 7.3

2. $\frac{r_1}{r_2} = \frac{x_k}{h}$; $r_1 = \frac{x_k}{h} r_2$

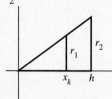

3. Rotate the cone 90° about the *x*-axis, then use the same similar triangles as in step 2.

4. Since the cross section is scaled both horizontally and vertically by a factor of $\frac{x_k}{h}$, the area is scaled by a factor of $\left(\frac{x_k}{h}\right)^2$. For example, a triangle of height *a* and base *b* which is scaled both horizontally and vertically by a factor of *r* will have area $\frac{1}{2}(rb)(ra) = \left(\frac{1}{2}ba\right)r^2$, which is the original area scaled by a factor of r^2.

5. The volume of the slab equals the area of its base times its height. Since the area of its base is $A\left(\frac{x_k}{h}\right)^2$, and its height is Δx, the volume of the slab is $A\left(\frac{x_k}{h}\right)^2 \Delta x$.

6. $\lim\limits_{n\to\infty} \sum\limits_{k=1}^{n} V_k = \lim\limits_{n\to\infty} \sum\limits_{k=1}^{n} A\left(\frac{x_k}{h}\right)^2 \Delta x$

$= \int_0^h \frac{A}{h^2} x^2 \, dx$

7. Since we are evaluating the integral with respect to *x*, $\frac{A}{h^2}$ is a constant, so we can move it outside of the integral by the Constant Multiple Rule for Definite Integrals.

8. $\frac{A}{h^2} \int_0^h x^2 \, dx = \frac{A}{h^2} \left[\frac{x^3}{3}\right]_0^h = \frac{A}{h^2} \times \frac{h^3}{3} = \frac{1}{3}Ah$

9. a. $V = \frac{1}{3}s^2 h$

   b. $V = \frac{\sqrt{3}}{12}s^2 h$

   c. $V = \frac{\sqrt{3}}{2}s^2 h$

Section 8.3

1. Let $f(x) = e^{-(x^2/2)}$ and $g(x) = e^{-x}$. *f* and *g* are continuous functions for all *x*, $0 \le f(x) \le g(x)$ for all $x \ge 2$, and $\int_2^{\infty} e^{-x} \, dx$ converges. So, by Theorem 3 (direct comparison test), $\int_2^{\infty} e^{-(x^2/2)} \, dx$ also converges.

Let $a = \int_2^{\infty} e^{-(x^2/2)} \, dx$. Since $f(x) = e^{-(x^2/2)}$ is an even function, $\int_{-\infty}^{-2} e^{-(x^2/2)} \, dx = a$. Now let $b = \int_{-2}^{2} e^{-(x^2/2)} \, dx$. We have $\int_{-\infty}^{\infty} e^{-(x^2/2)} \, dx = a + b + a = 2a + b$.

Therefore $\int_{-\infty}^{\infty} e^{-(x^2/2)} \, dx$ converges.

2. $\int_{-4}^{4} e^{-(x^2/2)} \, dx \approx 2.50646950$

$\int_{-6}^{6} e^{-(x^2/2)} \, dx \approx 2.50662827$

$\int_{-8}^{8} e^{-(x^2/2)} \, dx \approx 2.50662828$

3. $\int_{-40}^{40} e^{-(x^2/2)} \, dx \approx \int_{-60}^{60} e^{-(x^2/2)} \, dx$

$\approx \int_{-80}^{80} e^{-(x^2/2)} \, dx \approx 2.506628275.$

4. It appears that

$\lim\limits_{N\to\infty} \int_{-N}^{N} e^{-(x^2/2)} \, dx \approx 2.506628275.$

We cannot conclude that this is an exact value of the integral.

5. No

6. $(2.506628275)^2 = 6.283185307$

7. $\frac{6.283185307}{2} = 3.141592654$;

$\int_{-\infty}^{\infty} e^{-(x^2/2)} \, dx = \sqrt{2\pi}$

8. 0

9. 120 units wide

10. $e^{-60^2/2} \approx 0$

11. All 100 of the rectangles will have area $\approx 120 \cdot 0 = 0$; The sum is 0.

12. 150 rectangles would each be 80 units wide. 200 rectangles would each be 60 units wide. The MRAM sum would still be 0.

13. If all of the rectangles have a calculated height of zero, then the sum of all of the rectangle areas will also be zero.

1. $T_O(x) = x + \dfrac{x^3}{3!} + \dfrac{x^5}{5!} + \dfrac{x^7}{7!} + \cdots + \dfrac{x^{2n+1}}{(2n+1)!} + \cdots;\ T_E(x) = 1 + \dfrac{x^2}{2!} + \dfrac{x^4}{4!} + \dfrac{x^6}{6!} + \cdots + \dfrac{x^{2n}}{(2n)!} + \cdots$

2. $\dfrac{T(x) + T(-x)}{2} = \dfrac{\left(1 + x + \dfrac{x^2}{2!} + \dfrac{x^3}{3!} + \cdots + \dfrac{x^n}{n!} + \cdots\right) + \left(1 + (-x) + \dfrac{(-x)^2}{2!} + \dfrac{(-x)^3}{3!} + \cdots + (-1)^n\dfrac{(-x)^n}{n!} + \cdots\right)}{2}$

$$= \dfrac{\left(1 + x + \dfrac{x^2}{2!} + \dfrac{x^3}{3!} + \cdots\right) + \left(1 - x + \dfrac{x^2}{2!} - \dfrac{x^3}{3!} + \cdots\right)}{2}$$

$$= \dfrac{2 + \dfrac{2x^2}{2!} + \dfrac{2x^4}{4!} + \cdots}{2} = 1 + \dfrac{x^2}{2!} + \dfrac{x^4}{4!} + \cdots + \dfrac{x^{2n}}{(2n)!} + \cdots = T_E(x)$$

3. $\dfrac{T(x) - T(-x)}{2} = \dfrac{\left(1 + x + \dfrac{x^2}{2!} + \dfrac{x^3}{3!} + \cdots + \dfrac{x^n}{n!} + \cdots\right) - \left(1 + (-x) + \dfrac{(-x)^2}{2!} + \dfrac{(-x)^3}{3!} + \cdots + (-1)^n\dfrac{(-x)^n}{n!} + \cdots\right)}{2}$

$$= \dfrac{\left(1 + x + \dfrac{x^2}{2!} + \dfrac{x^3}{3!} + \cdots\right) - 1 + x - \dfrac{x^2}{2!} + \dfrac{x^3}{3!} + \cdots}{2}$$

$$= \dfrac{2x + \dfrac{2x^3}{3!} + \dfrac{2x^5}{5!} + \cdots}{2} = 1 + \dfrac{x^3}{3!} + \dfrac{x^5}{5!} + \cdots + \dfrac{x^{2n+1}}{(2n+1)!} + \cdots = T_O(x)$$

4. $T_E(x)$ is similar to $\cos x$ except that every other term in the expansion of $\cos x$ is negative.

5. $T_O(x)$ is similar to $\sin x$ except that every other term in the expansion of $\sin x$ is negative.

6. $\sinh x = \dfrac{e^x - e^{-x}}{2}$

7. $\dfrac{e^x + e^{-x}}{2} + \dfrac{e^x - e^{-x}}{2} = \dfrac{e^x + e^{-x} + e^x - e^{-x}}{2} = \dfrac{2e^x}{2} = e^x$

8. $\dfrac{f(x) + f(-x)}{2} + \dfrac{f(x) - f(-x)}{2} = \dfrac{f(x) + f(-x) + f(x) - f(-x)}{2} = \dfrac{2f(x)}{2} = f(x)$

Furthermore, $f_O(x) = \dfrac{f(x) - f(-x)}{2}$ is odd because $f_O(-x) = \dfrac{f(-x) - f(x)}{2} = -\dfrac{f(x) - f(-x)}{2} = -f_O(x)$, and

$f_E(x) = \dfrac{f(x) + f(-x)}{2}$ is even because $f_E(-x) = \dfrac{f(-x) + f(x)}{2} = \dfrac{f(x) + f(-x)}{2} = f_E(x)$.

9. $f_E(x) = \dfrac{f(x) + f(-x)}{2} = \dfrac{\dfrac{1}{1-x} + \dfrac{1}{1+x}}{2} = \dfrac{\dfrac{1+x}{(1+x)(1-x)} + \dfrac{1-x}{(1+x)(1-x)}}{2} = \dfrac{2}{1-x^2} \cdot \dfrac{1}{2} = \dfrac{1}{1-x^2}$

$f_O(x) = \dfrac{f(x) - f(-x)}{2} = \dfrac{\dfrac{1}{1-x} - \dfrac{1}{1+x}}{2} = \dfrac{\dfrac{1+x}{(1+x)(1-x)} - \dfrac{1-x}{(1+x)(1-x)}}{2} = \dfrac{2x}{1-x^2} \cdot \dfrac{1}{2} = \dfrac{x}{1-x^2}$

10. $\dfrac{x}{1-x^2} = x + x^3 + x^5 + x^7 + \cdots + x^{2n+1} + \cdots$

$\dfrac{1}{1-x^2} = 1 + x^2 + x^4 + x^6 + \cdots + x^{2n} + \cdots$

$\dfrac{1}{1-x} = 1 + x + x^2 + x^3 + x^4 + \cdots + x^n + \cdots$

11. $\ln(x+1) = x - \dfrac{x^2}{2} + \dfrac{x^3}{3} - \dfrac{x^4}{4} + \cdots + (-1)^{n-1}\dfrac{x^n}{n} + \cdots$

$$\ln \sqrt{1-x^2} = -\frac{x^2}{2} - \frac{x^4}{4} - \frac{x^6}{6} - \cdots - \frac{x^{2n}}{2n} - \cdots$$

$$\ln\left(\sqrt{\frac{1+x}{1-x}}\right) = x + \frac{x^3}{3} + \frac{x^5}{5} + \cdots + \frac{x^{2n-1}}{2n-1} + \cdots$$

Section 10.6

2. If n is odd, then there are n petals. If n is even, then there are $2n$ petals.
3. If n is odd, then each petal is traced twice over the interval $0 \le \theta \le 2\pi$. So, for all positive integers, n, there are $2n$ petals traced over the interval $0 \le \theta \le 2\pi$.
4. NINT$((2\sin(2x))^2, x, 0, 2\pi)/2 \approx 6.283185307$. We integrate over the interval $0 \le x \le 2\pi$ to include the entire graph.
5. 2π
6. There are three times as many petals, but the area is the same.
7. NINT$((2\sin(3x))^2, x, 0, \pi)/2 \approx 3.141592654$. We integrate over the interval $0 \le x \le \pi$ so that we include each petal only once. The exact area is π.
8. $A = \begin{cases} 2\pi, & n \text{ even} \\ \pi, & n \text{ odd} \end{cases}$

9. One petal is traced over the interval $0 \le \theta \le \frac{\pi}{n}$, so

$$A = \frac{1}{2}\int_0^{\pi/n} (2\sin(n\theta))^2 \, d\theta$$
$$= \frac{1}{2}\int_0^{\pi/n} 4\sin^2(n\theta) \, d\theta$$
$$= 2\int_0^{\pi/n} \sin^2(n\theta) \, d\theta$$

10. Let $u = n\theta$ and $du = n\,d\theta$.

So, $0 \le u \le \pi$ and $\frac{du}{n} = d\theta$.

$$2\int_0^{\pi/n} \sin^2(n\theta)\,d\theta = 2\int_0^{\pi} \sin^2(u)\frac{du}{n}$$
$$= \frac{2}{n}\int_0^{\pi} \sin^2(u)\,du.$$

11. The area of 1 petal is $\frac{2}{n}\int_0^{\pi} \sin^2(u)\,du = \frac{A}{n}$. If n is odd, there are n petals and the area is $n\left(\frac{A}{n}\right) = A$. If n is even, there are $2n$ petals and the area is $2n\left(\frac{A}{n}\right) = 2A$.

12. $A = 2\int_0^{\pi} \sin^2(u)\,du = 2\left[\frac{u}{2} - \frac{\sin 2u}{4}\right]_0^{\pi} = \pi.$

So, if n is odd the area is π, and if n is even the area is 2π.

Sample Advanced Placement Tests

AB: Section I Answers

1. C	2. E	3. C	4. A
5. B	6. C	7. A	8. B
9. E	10. A	11. D	12. B
13. B	14. E	15. D	16. C
17. A	18. A	19. D	20. D
21. B	22. E	23. C	24. C
25. E	26. E	27. C	28. B
29. B	30. A	31. E	32. C
33. E	34. D	35. E	36. B
37. B	38. D	39. B	40. A
41. D	42. B	43. D	44. A
45. D			

AB: Section II Answers

1. (a) $-2 < x < 3$

(b)
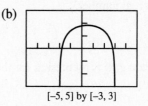
[−5, 5] by [−3, 3]

(c) $x = -2, x = 3$

(d) $\dfrac{-2x+1}{-x^2+x+6}$ or $\dfrac{2x-1}{x^2-x-6}$

(e) $f'(x) = 0$ at $x = 0.5$, so $f(x) \le \ln 6.25 \approx 1.833$.

2. (a) $2 - 5\pi\cos\pi t$

(b) $t^2 + \dfrac{5}{\pi}\cos\pi t - \dfrac{5}{\pi}$

(c) $0 < t < 0.885$ or $2.418 < t < 2.500$

(d) ≈ 4.658

3. (a) $(2, 8)$

(b) $\displaystyle\int_0^2 (4\sqrt[3]{4x} - x^3)\,dx = 8$

(c) $\displaystyle\int_0^8 \left(\sqrt[3]{y} - \frac{y^3}{256}\right) dy$

(d) $\displaystyle\pi\int_0^8 \left[(\sqrt[3]{y}+1)^2 - \left(\frac{y^3}{256}+1\right)^2\right] dy$

or $2\pi\displaystyle\int_0^2 (x+1)(4\sqrt[3]{4x} - x^3)\,dx$

4. (a) $64\pi h(t) + \dfrac{4}{3}\pi[r(t)]^3$

(b) Volume $= 64\pi(1 + \ln 24) \approx 840.048$ in^3 at $t = 23$ sec

(c) $-80\pi \approx -251.327$ in^3/sec

(d) Radius $= \sqrt[3]{48(18 - \ln 4)} \approx 9.273$ in.;

rate $= \dfrac{5}{[6(18 - \ln 4)]^{2/3}} \approx 0.233$ in./sec

5. (a) $-\dfrac{y + \dfrac{5}{2\sqrt{x}}}{x + 3y^2}$

(b) $y = -\dfrac{4}{7}x + \dfrac{15}{7}$

(c) 1.8

(d) $5\sqrt{0.6} + 0.6y + y^3 = 11; f(0.6) \approx 1.821$

(e) No; -0.1 is not in the domain of $f(x)$ because $\sqrt{-0.1}$ is not a real number.

6. (a) 5

(b) $-1 < x < 2$, since $g(x)$ is increasing for these values of x.

(c) $-3 + \displaystyle\int_0^x g(t)\, dt$

(d)

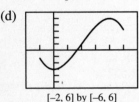

[−2, 6] by [−6, 6]

BC: Section I Answers

1. E	2. E	3. C	4. A
5. E	6. B	7. E	8. D
9. C	10. B	11. E	12. A
13. C	14. B	15. C	16. B
17. B	18. D	19. B	20. C
21. E	22. B	23. A	24. C
25. A	26. B	27. A	28. E
29. B	30. D	31. E	32. D
33. D	34. D	35. E	36. C
37. C	38. D	39. D	40. E
41. D	42. D	43. A	44. B
45. E			

BC: Section II Answers

1. (a) $\langle 75, 40 \rangle$; magnitude $= 85$

(b) 163 units

(c) $\dfrac{8}{3t}$

(d) $-\dfrac{8}{9t^4}$

2. (a) $(2, 8)$

(b) $\displaystyle\int_0^2 (4\sqrt[3]{4x} - x^3)\, dx = 8$

(c) $\displaystyle\int_0^8 \left(\sqrt[3]{y} - \dfrac{y^3}{256}\right) dy$

(d) $\pi\displaystyle\int_0^8 \left[(\sqrt[3]{y} + 1)^2 - \left(\dfrac{y^3}{256} + 1\right)^2\right] dy$ or

$2\pi\displaystyle\int_0^2 (x + 1)(4\sqrt[3]{4x} - x^3)\, dx$

3. (a) $64\pi h(t) + \dfrac{4}{3}\pi[r(t)]^3$

(b) $-80\pi \approx -251.327$ in^3/sec

(c) $\dfrac{5}{[6(18 - \ln 4)]^{2/3}} \approx 0.233$ in./sec

(d) Volume $= 64\pi(23 - \ln 24) \approx 3985.439$ in^3 at $t = 23$ sec

4. (a) $6 + 8x + 15x^2 + 8x^3$

(b) 8.264; maximum error is 0.005.

(c) $6x + 8x^3 + 15x^5 + 8x^7 + \cdots$

(d) $5 + 6x + 4x^2 + 5x^3 + 2x^4 + \cdots$

5. (a) Area $= \dfrac{1}{2}\displaystyle\int_0^{2\pi} r^2\, d\theta = 4.5\pi \approx 14.137$

(b) $\dfrac{k \sin k\theta \sin \theta - (2 + \cos k\theta) \cos \theta}{k \sin k\theta \cos \theta + (2 + \cos k\theta) \sin \theta}$

(c) $\dfrac{\pi}{4}$

6. (a) 8 　　　　 (b) 1

(c) $\dfrac{1}{9}g'\left(\dfrac{x}{3} + 2\right)$

(d) $x > 6$, since this is where $g\left(\dfrac{x}{3} + 2\right)$ is decreasing.

(e)

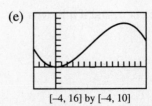

[−4, 16] by [−4, 10]